A Brief Introduction to John Calvin

A Brief Introduction to John Calvin

Christopher Elwood

WESTMINSTER
JOHN KNOX PRESS
LOUISVILLE · KENTUCKY

© 2017 Christopher Elwood

Previously published as *Calvin for Armchair Theologians* (Louisville, KY: Westminster John Knox Press, 2002).

First edition
Published by Westminster John Knox Press
Louisville, Kentucky

17 18 19 20 21 22 23 24 25 26—10 9 8 7 6 5 4 3 2 1

All rights reserved. No part of this book may be reproduced or transmitted in any form or by any means, electronic or mechanical, including photocopying, recording, or by any information storage or retrieval system, without permission in writing from the publisher. For information, address Westminster John Knox Press, 100 Witherspoon Street, Louisville, Kentucky 40202-1396. Or contact us online at www.wjkbooks.com.

Scripture quotations from the New Revised Standard Version of the Bible are copyright © 1989 by the Division of Christian Education of the National Council of the Churches of Christ in the U.S.A. and are used by permission.

Scripture quotations marked RSV are from the Revised Standard Version of the Bible, copyright © 1946, 1952, 1971, and 1973 by the Division of Christian Education of the National Council of the Churches of Christ in the U.S.A., and are used by permission.

Book design by Sharon Adams
Cover design by Allison Taylor

Library of Congress Cataloging-in-Publication Data

Names: Elwood, Christopher.
Title: A brief introduction to John Calvin / Christopher Elwood.
Description: Louisville, KY : Westminster John Knox Press, 2017. | Includes bibliographical references and index.
Identifiers: LCCN 2016041535 (print) | LCCN 2016042421 (ebook) | ISBN 9780664262242 (pbk. : alk. paper) | ISBN 9781611647860 (ebk.)
Subjects: LCSH: Calvin, Jean, 1509-1564.
Classification: LCC BX9418 .E49 2017 (print) | LCC BX9418 (ebook) | DDC 284/.2092 [B] --dc23
LC record available at https://lccn.loc.gov/2016041535

♾ The paper used in this publication meets the minimum requirements of the American National Standard for Information Sciences—Permanence of Paper for Printed Library Materials, ANSI Z39.48-1992.

Most Westminster John Knox Press books are available at special quantity discounts when purchased in bulk by corporations, organizations, and special-interest groups. For more information, please e-mail SpecialSales@wjkbooks.com.

For Izzy, and *all the others*

Contents

Preface	ix
Introduction	xi
1. Forming a Reformer	1
2. Struggle for the Light	10
3. Orienting Theology	19
4. Trials and Travail	62
5. Calvin's Children	71
Notes	87
Further Reading	89
Index	93

Preface

John Calvin—Protestant reformer of the sixteenth century, pastor of the church of Geneva, gifted interpreter of the Bible, theologian and educator, shaper of a rich and diverse theological and liturgical tradition known as Reformed Protestantism, influential theorist of the role of religion in relation to government and culture—was a complicated person. His approach to understanding God, the world, and human experience created possibilities for thinking and acting that would take his successors down diverse and often divergent paths. That, at least, is the thesis of this short exploration of the man and his thought.

The idea that Calvin is not simple but complex is not one you are likely to find in most popular presentations. It seems easy to find a two-dimensional Calvin, one we either enthusiastically embrace or summarily dismiss depending on our prior commitments. But a simple Calvin tends to be the product of casual acquaintance. What this introduction attempts to do is invite you into a closer reading, even as we move quickly across a wide span of Calvin's thinking, in the context of his life and his world, as well as the multiple legacies of his thought. It is an invitation, then, to begin to get to know a figure often misunderstood. That invitation is based on an assumption: there is a richer texture in Calvin's world of thought and spiritual practice than you might initially suspect.

And so, at the outset, I begin with an appeal to you, the reader, to at least temporarily suspend your skepticism. There are many like me, and not by any means all rabid Calvin aficionados, who have found in him a worthy and instructive conversation partner. Even where we vehemently disagree with him, we find we have learned something by engaging the questions he took up and looking from his vantage point at the sources of faith and reflection that continue to guide our paths. You might find him worth your while too.

The movement of religious reform pioneered by Martin Luther in Germany, carried through in Swiss cities by Huldrych Zwingli and others, and later championed by Calvin especially in France and Geneva has reached the ripe old age of five hundred. We might suggest that this longevity is proof that a tradition of Protestantism stemming from these folk of the 1500s has not only staying power but also the integrity and creativity to continue to guide communities of faith. But that would be a little simpleminded. Instead, it might be better to pose some questions: What has this tradition, in its various permutations, achieved—for good and for ill? How might our wrestling with this tradition help equip us for the challenges and opportunities of our time? Through this guide to Calvin, I hope that you will be better equipped to take up questions like these, or at least find an opening to further encounters to help you think more deeply about this tradition in relation to today's world.

I could not have produced this book without help from many corners. I'm grateful to those who helped me conceive the project initially, especially Nick Street; to those who assisted with the early writing and the form of the text, including Emily Rodgers Bisset, David Cantrell, Amy Plantinga Pauw, Johanna W. H. van Wijk-Bos; as well as to my colleagues in theological studies and the many passionate students and readers who have helped train me to see more clearly as a historical theologian and who encouraged me to try to match clarity of vision to simplicity of expression. My life partner, Narges Moshiri, might have preferred me to concentrate on "one of those nice medieval mystics" (as one of her mentors, Annemarie Schimmel, once put it) instead of the seemingly forbidding reformer of Geneva. But she was a tolerant helpmeet, without whom all these labors would have amounted to very little. Her too-brief life taught me more of spiritual value than any other mortal example, and I am deeply in her debt in more ways than I can say. Our unruly brood also needs to be acknowledged, as Josephine, Isabelle, Danny, Alfonso, Alfredo, Mateo, and all the rest have somehow managed to keep me grounded through this and other projects. This one is dedicated, with my love, to them all; but Isabelle moves to the top of the list this time.

Introduction

You have been invited to a dinner party, and after accepting the invitation, you discover some eminent cultural figure will also attend. As you make your way to the event, you turn to your companion, asking for a quick snapshot of this person, knowing as you do that he has a reputation but unsure about exactly what that reputation is and whether or not it is deserved. You would like to avoid embarrassment, either in sidebar exchanges with your fellow guests or on the chance that you are drawn into conversation with the man himself. Whether or not you have any background in scouting, your motto is, "Be prepared."

In the same way, naturally you want some basic thumbnail sketch of the subject of this book, to prepare you for what might be coming in the chapters ahead. Fair enough.

So who was John Calvin?

A humorless killjoy, determined to put an end to fun in any form?

The fashioner of a brand of Christian sadomasochism for the modern age?

The dyspeptic tyrant of Geneva who tried to bend a whole society to his will?

An early proponent of a feel-good philosophy of life?

Well, none of these exactly.

John Calvin was a religious reformer and one of the most influential Christian theologians of the Reformation period and, indeed, of the modern world. His influence was so great that by the time he died, in 1564, the hundreds of thousands of Protestants who were attracted to his view of Christian teaching had come to be called Calvinists. In the middle and late sixteenth century, Calvinism was the fastest growing form of

Protestant Christianity. Calvinist churches sprang up all over Europe—from Poland and Hungary to the Netherlands and Scotland—and in the new European settlements in America. Calvinism would leave an indelible imprint on the religion and culture of Europe, North America, South Africa, and other parts of the world where immigrants brought Calvin's theology and tried to fashion communities that reflected God's intention for human life. According to some historians, the modern world itself—its scientific ideas, its economic and political theories, its attitudes toward culture—is not understandable apart from the contributions and the impact of Calvin and his followers.

Calvin was a much more complicated person than most popular caricatures of him suggest. He was a Frenchman (his first name was *Jean* and the family name was originally *Cauvin*). Fiercely devoted to his homeland, he was forced to live most of his life outside of France. As a religious refugee, he cultivated friendships with people throughout Europe and developed an international outlook. He was by nature shy and retiring, more comfortable with private study than with the exposure of public life. And yet as a church reformer, and a politician of sorts, he led a stormy life and one very much in public view. Unlike some of his famous contemporaries, Calvin didn't tell us much about his inner life. And because of this reserve, he is a difficult person to get to know. He seems to elude attempts to sum him up in a simple way. But let us try to get better acquainted by starting with his formative settings—where he came from, his early influences, and the world of ideas that shaped who he was to become.

Chapter One

Forming a Reformer

On July 10, 1509, Gérard Calvin and Jeanne Le Franc had a baby boy, their second. They were a middle-class family in Noyon, a small city in the northern French province of Picardy. Gérard was a notary in the employ of the Cathedral chapter of Noyon. This position gave him useful contacts with the most influential institution in the region—the church— and with some of the more influential families of the city. The baby boy, Jean, turned out to be smart, and when the time came, his father used his connections to get him a good education. In Noyon he learned alongside the children of the aristocratic Hangest family and formed lasting friendships and a lifelong affinity for cultured society. His education continued at the University of Paris. Gérard intended the bright boy for a career in the church, where he would likely make a name for himself. (As a bishop? Or cardinal? Perhaps pope?!) We don't know what Jean's mother intended for him. She died when he was about five years old.

It was in Paris that the young Calvin first encountered the wider world of ideas that would so profoundly shape his way of thinking. He began the basic course of studies in Latin grammar, ending up at the Collège de Montaigu, which had a reputation for being especially hard on its students. Its pedagogy featured regular beatings and the formation of character through bad food, unhealthy water, and squalid living conditions. Calvin never complained. As a model student, he probably escaped the harshest treatment meted out to those less fortunately endowed.

In the early 1520s, when Calvin began his studies, the University of Paris was one of the main centers of theological conservatism in Europe. When the ideas of a certain Martin Luther (1483–1546) began to filter into France from Germany, the Paris Faculty of Theology was one of the very first to denounce them. This faculty—known as the Sorbonne—was the protector of a traditional form of theology called scholasticism. In addition to Luther, the Sorbonne also was quick to denounce other reformers whose writings either directly or by implication rejected traditional forms of theological thinking. Although Calvin was not a theology student in Paris, he certainly must have been exposed to some of the Lutheran ideas that had made their way into the city, as well as to the attacks the Parisian theologians made on this new heresy.

Since he was bound for the priesthood, it would have been natural for Calvin to make his way to the Sorbonne and a course of theological study. But his father, who was in the midst of a quarrel with the church authorities back home, changed his mind about his son's career and saved him from ordination. Instead, Gérard decided that his son would go into law. So, always obedient to his father's wishes, Calvin took the main road south from Paris to Orléans where he began to study law under the celebrated scholar Pierre de l'Estoile (1480–1537). Then he headed further south to the Academy of Bourges. Andrea Alciati (1492–1550), an Italian humanist teacher of the law and a star to rival l'Estoile, had just arrived in Bourges, and Calvin wanted to see firsthand what all the fuss was about. At this point, his studies were as much literary and historical as they were legal, which is to say that Calvin had been bitten by the bug of Renaissance humanism.

What Was Humanism?

The Renaissance humanism of the fifteenth and sixteenth centuries was not what most people think of when they use the term "humanism" today. It was a movement of cultural and intellectual reform that started in Italy with the teachers of the *studia humanitatis*—the liberal arts—and gradually moved northward. When Calvin was in school, humanism was a strong force in intellectual circles in France. It was favored by the king, Francis I (1494–1547). His sister Marguerite of Navarre (1492–1549), who protected humanist reformers in her court from their conservative opponents (such as those at the Sorbonne), was a special enthusiast. The most famous humanist of Calvin's time was Desiderius Erasmus (1469–1536). The most celebrated French humanists of the period were Jacques Lefèvre d'Étaples (c. 1450–1536) and Guillaume Budé (1468–1540). Both Erasmus and Lefèvre were well-known for their biblical scholarship.

Humanists were interested in reviving the literary values of classical antiquity. They believed that the medieval period had been a time of decline. The Latin language had become corrupted, along with public institutions such as the church, and the moral life both of the clergy and of ordinary laypeople left a good deal to be desired. Humanists thought that by reforming language and the process of education and promoting eloquent expression they would improve spiritual and moral life as well. They championed the study of classical rhetoric—the art of eloquent expression for the purpose of persuasion—in order to improve their society on many fronts.

The humanist slogan was *ad fontes*—"back to the sources"—meaning the original sources of European, classical culture. Humanist legal scholars such as Alciati intended to go back to the sources by using sophisticated literary and historical methods to establish the original forms of Roman law and to show how the law had changed and developed. For those who saw themselves specifically as Christian humanists, going back to the sources meant returning to the earliest Christian writings, particularly the texts of the Bible; not the Vulgate—the Latin translation that had become the standard Bible of the West—but the original texts in their original languages. The oldest manuscripts needed to be studied, and new translations and interpretations needed to be produced using the best literary methods available.

Humanism was very exciting to many educated people in Europe as it seemed to herald a new time of enlightened thinking. But, since it implied a criticism of the prevailing theological and ecclesiastical culture (one that, according to the humanists, had perpetuated superstition and ignorance), it posed a threat to those who were wedded to the older, scholastic forms of theology. This is one of the reasons conservatives in the University of Paris were suspicious of the humanists.

In catching the fever of humanism, Calvin was clearly not a conservative Catholic. But being a humanist did not mean that one was not a Catholic at all. His father had gotten into trouble with the church authorities in Noyon, but there is no strong evidence that Calvin himself had become disaffected with traditional Catholic faith in his student years. Of course, some of his associates had Lutheran ideas, including Melchior Wolmar (d. 1561), who taught him Greek at Bourges. And it is possible that Calvin had come to entertain some of these ideas himself. Certainly by his early twenties, when he had completed his legal studies and was moving in humanist circles in Paris, he had come to be very familiar with Martin Luther and a number of others who were talking about a movement they called a reformation of the church.

Luther and the Reformation Movement

Luther was an Augustinian monk in Germany who, beginning with criticisms of scholastic theology and current church practices such as the granting of indulgences (which forgave church-imposed works of penance required to satisfy the terms of sacramental confession), came to reject entirely the power of the pope to direct what Christians should believe. Luther and his followers insisted that the Bible alone should determine right belief. When Luther read the Bible, and particularly the writings of Paul, he found the key to the Christian message: the teaching of justification by faith alone.

Luther's schema went something like this:

- We are all sinful.
- God justifies, or saves, those who have faith in God, through the work of Jesus Christ.
- This justification is not a reward for the struggle to be good.
- So being a Christian is not, first and foremost, a matter of what one does.
- It is about accepting what God has done for you.
- That acceptance is faith.

For Luther, this was what the Bible taught. Human beings are saved by God's grace, not by their own meritorious works. Of course, Luther drew on sources other than the Bible, including the writings of Augustine (354–430). Augustine, the great doctor of grace, had insisted in the early fifth century (against the British monk Pelagius) that humans have no capacity to will and to do what is good unless God reorders their will. Luther's understanding of justification reflected his and a number of his contemporaries' rediscovery of Augustine's emphasis on the priority of God's grace.

Luther also taught the priesthood of all believers (or all baptized Christians). Christianity should not create a spiritual elite—the priesthood as opposed to laypeople—because all Christians are part of Christ's body and can pray for one another, hear another's confession of sin, preach, and teach one another about the good news of God's grace. Ministers or preachers of the Word hold an office the church still needs, but the clergy are not superior to or set apart from the laity.

These teachings (but particularly his challenge to the pope's authority) got Luther excommunicated, declared a heretic by the church and an outlaw by the secular government in Germany. Nevertheless, many people were won over by his ideas, including a number of local governments and rulers within the many, more or less autonomous, territories of Germany. In Switzerland, similar ideas were being taught by Huldrych Zwingli (1484–1531) and some other reformers (who combined Luther's emphasis on the centrality of the Bible and the priority of grace with their commitments to humanist values). In addition to the territories won over by Luther's teachings, a number of prominent Swiss and South German cities, closer to Zwingli's sphere of influence, were converted to a movement that would in time come to be called Protestantism or (because of its emphasis on the gospel) the evangelical movement. People at this time thought of it as a movement to reform the church according to the word of God. Most did not think they were creating a new church. They simply wanted to reform a church whose abuses (the buying and selling of church offices, the holding of multiple offices by single individuals, poor clergy preparation and performance of basic clerical duties) had, in their view, compromised its claim to represent adequately the body of Christ. But, in fact, adopting these reforming ideas effectively involved breaking relations with Rome and with the church headed by the pope.

An Unexpected Turnabout

Just when Calvin came over to these views of reformation is not terribly clear. Possibly when he was a law student and possibly in the period after his studies were completed he experienced what he later called "a sudden conversion" or "an unexpected turnabout" (depending on how you translate his Latin). If this is a conversion experience of the sort the apostle Paul experienced on the road to Damascus (flashes of light, a voice from heaven) or of the kind effected by later revivalistic preaching during the Great Awakening (warmings of the heart, intense emotionalism), Calvin never told anyone about it. A more likely scenario is that over time he came to be aware that God was turning him away from one kind of religious orientation (one that he would later associate with the ignorance and error of popery and idolatry) and toward another (the evangelism that was preached by Luther and others). When Calvin later spoke about a "conversion" or "turnabout," he was less interested in specifying the character of an interior experience than in conveying a message that had come to be at the heart of his mature theology: What happens to us in life is the result of God's working. Calvin came at some point in his youth or young adulthood to the truth taught in the Bible and its good news of

God's grace, and he left behind the practices of popular Catholicism and the religious thought forms in which he was reared. To his thinking, it was not Calvin that caused this; it was God.

The way for this conversion had been prepared by his intellectual interests in humanism. It had been prepared by some of those Lutheran ideas he had absorbed. It had also been prepared by France's own home-grown version of reformation, a movement influenced by the humanist Jacques Lefèvre d'Étaples. Lefèvre was a somewhat more sedate personality than the more notorious German reformer. And, unlike Luther, he was never declared a heretic, and so his followers were not forced to choose between reformation and the papal church—at least not at first. Calvin eventually did have to choose—and his choice was forced by some uncomfortable episodes in Paris in the years 1533–1534, when Calvin was a young Christian humanist about town and probably also a recent convert to the reformation movement.

Humanist Scholar or Reformer on the Run?

It was in this period, when Calvin was in his early twenties, that he had to make some momentous decisions. Who was he going to be? Here he was, with his law degree and some pretty good scholarly credentials. What was he going to do with these? He tried his hand at some writing and published a commentary on the Roman philosopher Seneca's treatise *On Clemency*, but it didn't make a tremendous splash in the world of letters. It seems Calvin's hand began to be forced by his associations. In 1533, his good friend Nicholas Cop was installed as the new rector of the University of Paris. In the All Saints' Day service (on November 1), Cop, whose humanist and reform-minded orientation reflected Calvin's thinking at the time, gave an address that sounded just enough like Luther, or maybe Erasmus or Lefèvre, to make the conservatives in Paris angry. In the wake of reactionary attempts at retribution, Calvin (who *might* have had a hand in writing the address) got out of town quickly. The atmosphere in Paris was becoming a little too hot for anyone whose ideas might be labeled Lutheran. Even Francis I, who had initially supported the humanists, seemed to be turning decisively against anything that smacked of heresy.

And so Calvin began a period of moving about, lying low, and keeping a good distance from Paris. He visited with the reformer Lefèvre at the court of Marguerite of Navarre, perhaps to discuss the steps he ought to take. In May 1534, he went back home to Noyon to resign the last of the church appointments (which were what we might think of as scholarships) whose earnings had helped to support his education and his scholarly pursuits. It may be that this is the point marking his decisive break with his Catholic past.

A break of an equally decisive sort happened because of what occurred on the night of October 17, 1534. In Paris and several of the larger cities and towns of France, a network of Protestant activists secretly posted placards that denounced Catholic "abuses," focusing on the central Catholic rite, the Mass, and denouncing as idolatry the Catholic theology of the eucharist. Francis I, who woke the next morning to find one of these posters on his bedroom door, was not amused. The content and the tone of the placard signaled a much more militant approach to reform than he was comfortable with. The king was not inclined to tolerate what he regarded as a sacrilegious assault on the church and the faith of his kingdom. Because several of the usual suspects were rounded up and burned as heretics, Calvin felt it would be wise this time not merely to get out of town but to remove himself to another country. He arrived in the Swiss city of Basel in January 1535.

Exile and a "Short Little Book"

Basel had adopted the Reformation in 1525 and was a favorite haunt of a number of humanists. (Erasmus lived there on and off in the 1520s and 1530s.) It was a good place for Calvin to do some writing. And now that he had clearly broken with the conservative orthodoxy that was currently being enforced in France and had moved into safe territory, he could write openly about his newly formed religious orientation.

And that is what he did. He set to work on a short (six chapters) summary of evangelical faith that would bring to light the essence of the Christian message contained in the Bible, a message he believed had been obscured by much of the institutional practice of the church and that now was being recovered in the Reformation movement. He dedicated the work to Francis I and addressed a letter to him that served as a preface to the text. In the letter, Calvin argued that the Protestants or evangelicals in France, who were currently being persecuted, were not dangerous to the state and were not corrupters of the church and Christian faith. Instead, they followed the true, biblical faith, the faith that the ancient catholic and apostolic church had held. The body of his text can be read as a continuation of the argument he began in the letter of dedication. The title Calvin gave to this book, *Christianae religionis institutio*, has come down to us in English as *Institutes of the Christian Religion*. But a more accurate translation might read something like *Formation in Christian Piety*.

This first major work of Calvin's gave him a favorable reputation among the international community of reform-minded people because it seemed to be a highly literate, comprehensive, and theologically adept presentation of the evangelical faith. With the elegance of a writer trained in humanist styles of effective communication and eschewing the dense philosophical method of scholastic theology, the young scholar had shown a capacity to bring clarity to the complexity of Christian truth. Calvin argued his points persuasively to his many audiences:

- to the opponents of the Protestants in his native country;
- to Francis I and others in power responsible for a policy of repression;
- to the community of Protestants suffering under the effects of this policy;
- and to a larger audience of persons not yet committed to one or another religious position but who were searching for a window on truth in disorienting times.

"The Times They Are a-Changin'"

Like many of his contemporaries, Calvin believed that the time he lived in was "a most unhappy age." Throughout his life he reflected on the state of the world in terms like the following: "Look at how nothing in the world ever lasts. Look at how everything is in constant turmoil. Look at how people are suddenly reduced from riches to rags. . . . What do we find in the world today, except trouble everywhere? If we find a place to rest, what assurance have we that we can remain there? Where can you find some small corner of the earth that has been at peace for any significant length of time?"[1]

At first glance, it is hard to see the reason for such a negative outlook. France in the early sixteenth century suffered less from war than in the previous century, Northern Europe was just beginning to enjoy the cultural rebirth of the Renaissance, the population was well on the way to recovering from the earlier ravages of the black death (which first struck Europe in the middle of the fourteenth century), and the economy was not bad. It was, however, a time of extraordinarily rapid change. Not only would this century see the greatest disruption in religious life ever experienced—Reformation movements tore into bits the formerly unified, catholic church (and in the process severely strained social relations)—there would also be unusual economic pressures (e.g., extremely high inflation reducing everyone's buying power, a long and steady drop in real wages). There would be regular threats to political stability with revolutionary movements cropping up from time to time (some of these inspired by the religious turmoil of the time). Calvin's own country, France, would descend into civil war at the end of his life and not emerge into a period of peace until more than three decades after his death. And the steady migration of rural populations into cities unprepared for rapid growth would lead to increases in urban poverty and crime.

Many people knew that an old world was disappearing and suspected that a new one was on its way. But there was no agreement about what that world would or should look like. One thing most people could agree on was that the present world was in disarray, with old verities challenged everywhere and chaos threatening to bring the earth to an abrupt, apocalyptic end. The new intellectual and religious movements of Calvin's day contributed to this sense of disconcertingly rapid change. But, of course, they were also attempting to address constructively concerns about the changes in society. Calvin's aim as he put pen to paper was to help find some order and light in a confusing time.

When he put the finishing touches on his *Institutes* and handed it over to his publisher, Calvin began looking about for a more permanent setting for his work. He spent a few months at the court of the Duchess of Ferrara in Italy. She was a member of the French royal family who was sympathetic to Protestants, and Calvin might have hoped to find gainful employment with her. When that plan failed, he headed back to Noyon in France for a brief visit to wrap up some family business before heading for the German Protestant city of Strasbourg. Calvin had several good friends there, the city had a small French Protestant community, and there was reason to hope he might put his skills to use in an agreeable environment. Calvin set out in July 1536. But he found he couldn't go to Strasbourg directly. There was a war between France and the German emperor, and the positions of the troops in the borderlands meant he would have to take a detour through the city of Geneva.

Chapter Two

Struggle for the Light

Two Destinies Colliding: Calvin and Geneva

Calvin, strolling through the gate known as the Porte Neuve and into the walled city, thought of this as a short layover. But he soon found it was easier to get into Geneva than to get out. That is because Calvin met Guillaume Farel there.

Farel (1489–1565) had once been a protégé of the mild-mannered Lefèvre but had gone on to become a fiery preacher of the gospel in French-speaking Switzerland. He had been the chief Protestant preacher in Geneva since 1532, when he first arrived in the city to rant against the city's Catholic establishment and advocate Protestant reform. When Farel learned that a capable young French scholar had ventured inside the city walls, he turned his fire on him, urging him to stay and join his ministry in Geneva and warning him that God's curse would follow him if he turned down the invitation. Calvin, who had in mind for himself a quiet life of scholarship, was reluctant to stay in Geneva and undertake a public ministry (probably especially because of the prospect of a partnership with the explosive Farel). But he feared God's curse—and probably Farel's too. He accepted the invitation.

Geneva at the time was a newly independent republic. It had adopted the Reformation just a few months before Calvin's arrival, at the same time that it won its political freedom. Having been ruled by its bishop, and for more than a century also under the control of the Duchy of Savoy (its powerful neighbor to the south), Geneva had managed to free itself of all external rulers by an alliance with the Swiss city of Bern (the primary military power to the east). The revolution of 1535–1536 was the culmination of a decades-long quest for autonomy by some of its most prominent citizens. The bishop was put to flight and his executive power was taken over by a series of citizen-elected councils, headed up by the twenty-five member Small Council, whose members were known as the city magistrates.

When Geneva's citizenry voted in May 1536 to adopt the Reformation ("to live henceforward according to the gospel") they sent out of the city all the Catholic clergy who could not live in the new religious climate. This left the city with a serious shortage of clergy and effectively without a church, if by church we mean a functioning ecclesiastical structure. The magistrates engaged a few Protestant preachers to hold services of worship, but there was no constitution to regulate worship and other practical matters of the church's life. Part of the job of Farel and Calvin, as they saw it, was to build a church. And that is what they set about doing in the first few years. Farel created a confession to summarize the new form of faith adopted by the city, while Calvin wrote a catechism to help the populace, especially children, learn the basic doctrines. He also set his hand to work on a church order—guidelines or rules for the functioning of the church. But these early years were complicated by the fact that the two preachers and the city magistrates had conflicting visions of the way the church should operate.

In 1937, an American named Dale Carnegie wrote a bestseller called *How to Win Friends and Influence People*. In 1991, some other Americans named Roger Fisher and William Ury wrote another bestseller titled *Getting to Yes: Negotiating Agreement without Giving In*. It is a pity that Calvin was unable to dip into these texts, as they might have given him some ideas about how to approach Geneva's new rulers. As it was, both he and Farel were completely inept when it came to courting persons with whom they found themselves in disagreement. They were both committed to designing a church in which the pastors would have a significant amount of control, especially over such things as church discipline and the celebration of the Lord's Supper. The magistrates, on the other hand, having worked for some time to rid their city of foreign tyranny, were wary of giving their foreign pastors too much authority. According to them, the pastors would have to do what the magistrates told them to do. The church would be controlled by the state. What ensued was disaster. Calvin and Farel were already unpopular with many Genevans for requiring that everyone attend worship services and for refusing to serve Communion to unrepentant sinners. When they dug in their heels and would not submit to the magistrates' plan for a church under state control, the Small Council sent them packing. On Easter Sunday 1538, Calvin was on the road again.

An Interim in Strasbourg and a Second Try in Geneva

So Calvin finally made his way to his original destination, Strasbourg, where (by his account) he spent a very pleasant few years as pastor to the French Reformed congregation, as a teacher in Strasbourg's Latin school, and as a writer on behalf of the evangelical movement. He enjoyed the company of Strasbourg's team of reformers, including Martin Bucer (1491–1551), Wolfgang Capito (1478–1541), and Jean Sturm (1507–1589), and learned a great deal from their ecclesiastical practice and scholarly example. He also got married. Under pressure from friends and colleagues to do what every Protestant ought to do (the Catholic ideal of clerical celibacy now being regarded as unnatural, unevangelical, and impractical), Calvin agreed to marry the widow Idelette de Bure—when she consented to have him. And although he believed himself to be not entirely well suited to married life, he seems to have been as happy with this arrangement as he was with his general state of affairs in the comparatively calm environment of Strasbourg.

But the respite from the turmoil of life in Geneva was not to last long. In 1541, after a political upheaval, the Genevan magistrates, now suspecting that they had been a little too hasty in giving him the boot, succeeded in luring Calvin back to their city. They agreed (in principle) to his condition that a system be set up for ordering the church along the lines he envisioned, but they left the details of this to be worked out later. And so when Calvin returned to the city in September, he immediately set to work on a document, the *Ecclesiastical Ordinances*, that would serve as a constitution for the church. It was to be an ordered church, with its own system of discipline. In Calvin's design, church ministry would be exercised in four offices.

- *Pastors* would proclaim the Word and administer the sacraments.
- *Doctors* would be responsible for the instruction of the faithful and the theological education of those preparing for ministry.
- *Elders* would have oversight of the moral life of the community. They would provide for Christian discipline by meeting regularly

with the pastors in a church court called a consistory, the forum for reviewing all cases of irregular behavior.
- Finally, *deacons* would care for the poor and the sick, disbursing funds to the indigent in an early modern version of social welfare.

When the magistrates ratified Calvin's ordinances, making only minor changes to them, it would seem that Calvin's triumph in Geneva was complete. But nothing was quite so simple in that city amid the Alps. Although Calvin had thought he had secured for the church the right to discipline its members without meddling from the civil government, some members of the Small Council had other views. Most (though not all) agreed that the consistory could discipline an obstinate sinner by barring him from the celebration of the Lord's Supper. But could the magistrates vote to overrule the consistory's decision? Many Genevans, especially those unhappy with their treatment by the consistory, thought they could. (Calvin called these people "Libertines," implying that they wanted freedom to indulge their many vices.) Many of the magistrates also believed they had this power. But Calvin was resolute and (as always) unyielding: Church discipline was a matter for the church and not the state. The pastors and the consistory (in which Calvin himself was a prominent presence) controlled access to Holy Communion.

In addition to his political struggles, Calvin also experienced deep personal sadness. Idelette had a very difficult pregnancy, gave birth prematurely, and the baby, whom they named Jacques, did not survive. Idelette never fully recovered her health. After several years of decline, she died on March 29, 1549. Calvin was devastated, deprived, as he told a friend, "of my excellent life companion, who, if misfortune had come, would have been my willing companion not only in exile and sorrow, but even in death." It was "a very cruel thing for me," he admitted, in the midst of praying for God to strengthen him. In keeping with the counsel he had given others, even in the face of this blow he continued to trust that God "relieves the broken, strengthens the weak, and renews those who are weary."[2]

So the sailing was not so smooth in Geneva for Calvin. He continued to butt heads with the magistrates and with elements in the population who resented his preaching and his policies. Shouting matches in Geneva's narrow streets between Calvin and some person he had managed to offend were not uncommon in these years. Not having benefited from the wisdom of Dale Carnegie, the foreign pastor often acted in high-handed ways, without sensitivity to local customs or concerns. He seems not to have been able to appreciate that for many Genevans the abrupt shift from Catholic to Protestant practices, from the faith of their grandparents to a new religious outlook, would be a painful process that might require from the pastors some patience and understanding. Instead, Calvin viewed all resistance as willfulness and wicked obstinacy. Geneva was, in his view, "a perverse and unhappy nation" full of "perverse and wicked" people. (This explains why he found it hard to get along with some of them.) Had he written a memoir of his Genevan ministry in this period, he might have titled it *How to Lose Friends and Alienate People*.

Calvin, however, did not lose all support in Geneva. When persecution of Protestants in France led to an enormous wave of immigration in the 1550s, the influx of refugees from Calvin's homeland bolstered his position in significant ways. But it also increased tension between local Genevans and the newly arrived French. Already despised by some for what they took to be arrogance, suspected in some quarters of wanting to make himself bishop and rule in Geneva as the old bishops had, Calvin became the target of a good deal of anti-French feeling. Those who had argued that the church should be subservient to the state began to feel that the question of church-state relations was especially critical when virtually *all* the pastors and more and more of their neighbors were French! Yes, on the upside you did have all those brioches and éclairs. But what of Genevan liberty?! Suddenly the question was not simply, "How will the church manage its affairs?" but, "Will free Genevans lose their freedom to the French?"

Matters came to a head in 1555 when Calvin's chief opponents, led by a certain Ami Perrin (the head of the party Calvin called "Libertines"), struck out (awkwardly) against this state of affairs. Charged with treason and attempting to take power by force, they were arrested, tried, and punished severely (banishment for some, execution for a few). The event marked the evaporation of opposition to Calvin and his policies. Now Calvin had finally triumphed.

The victory of 1555 gave Calvin considerable authority in Geneva. But contrary to the expectations of some, he did not try to make himself bishop. And he never exercised civil power. Although after 1555 he was greatly respected by those who served on the Small Council and his advice was generally (though not always) heeded, he was never more than a pastor and the designated head of the Company of Pastors. Popular conceptions of Geneva as a theocracy and of Calvin as its dictator therefore need some revision.

Post Tenebras Lux

Calvin's ministry in Geneva had many more features than is suggested by this account of his struggle for a disciplined church. He preached regularly (frequently as often as once a day). He had the usual pastoral visits. He lectured on the Bible. But his ministry as a whole was directed toward a project he called "reformation." At the end of his life, he noted that when he arrived in 1536, there was no reformation in Geneva, even though the majority of citizens approved the evangelical faith. Reformation, in Calvin's understanding, involved something more radical than a change in ideology. It could not be achieved simply with institutional tinkering. It was a matter of the whole of life, and it extended to everyone in society. It was a project that aimed at a complete reorientation of religious and civic life in accordance with what God discloses as God's will in Scripture, the building of what later Calvinists would call "a holy commonwealth," a "perfect school of Christ," a "city on a hill."

One account of this vision can be seen on Geneva's official seal. The coat of arms, in addition to the older, standard symbols of church and state (the imperial eagle, the episcopal key), includes two elements, introduced in the wake of the Reformation, that express a distinctive religious consciousness. A rising sun with the Greek letters IHS, an abbreviation for Jesus, echoes Calvin's interpretation of Malachi 4:2: "But for you who revere my name the sun of righteousness shall rise, with healing in its wings." The motto on the emblem makes the message plain: *Post tenebras lux*—"After darkness, light." According to the designers of the newly adopted coat of arms, Geneva had emerged from a time of darkness, in which Christ's truth was obscured by "papist superstitions," into a time of light, achieved through the preaching of Christ and the word of God.

For Calvin, however, light would not come without hard work. The project of building the church in Geneva was not to be confused with a declaration that light had come. Here he parted company with those who thought it enough to introduce the preaching of the evangelical message. In contrast to his Lutheran friends, who believed that a church existed wherever God's word "is taught purely," Calvin insisted that the word be "purely preached *and heard*." The addition of the last two words meant that a truly reformed church had to have not just a competent preacher but an attentive audience, and an audience upon whom the word had an effect. This is one reason why Calvin expended so much energy trying to institute effective means of discipline in the church. Discipline was a tool pastors and other church leaders could use to gauge the effect of preaching and teaching, to make instruction more effective in people's lives, and so to promote the building of a city of God.

A Toolbox for Reformation

But Calvin devised other tools to contribute to the project of the reformation of life and for propagating a Reformed movement, tools that would serve not only Geneva but the church beyond—in France, elsewhere in Europe, and (in time) even in the New World. Some of the most important of these were:

Tool 1: Designing Reformed Catechesis, Worship, and Church Structure

Calvin helped to create a culture of Reformed religion through his many writings. Some of the most influential of these were the writings intended to instruct the laity. Calvin wrote the hugely successful *Genevan Catechism* in 1542. It became the main vehicle for introducing Protestants to the Reformed faith not only in Geneva but in all French-speaking areas. He also shaped Reformed worship. His liturgies were widely used, and he assisted the collection and publishing of translations of the Psalms in verse form. The Genevan Psalter was one of the most popular songbooks of the sixteenth century and served as the hymnbook for virtually all Reformed congregations. A Reformed culture was also advanced through Calvin's pioneering means of structuring the church. The Genevan system of deliberative bodies (a consistory, a company of pastors) and practices of mutual admonition and support were adapted for use in larger territories (such as France, Scotland, and the Netherlands) where the hierarchy of church courts that typifies a Presbyterian system of church government first emerged (with congregational consistories or sessions, regional classes or presbyteries, and a national synod or general assembly).

Tool 2: Developing Pastors

The task of reforming all of life was also served through cultivating and training strong candidates for ministry. Calvin helped to do this by trying to attract the most able pastors to Geneva. But he also did it by raising the standards of ministerial preparation and introducing a high quality of theological education. Through his own lecturing and by establishing the Genevan Academy of higher learning, he saw to it that Reformed ministers would have a strong, liberal education, gain the skills necessary to read the Bible in its original languages and interpret it using the best philological techniques, and be adequately grounded in the Christian theological tradition. Forming capable pastors was to be a significant part of reforming the church and spreading Calvin's vision of reformation.

Tool 3: Aiding the Interpretation of Scripture

For the able Reformed pastor, but also to aid the general Christian reader, Calvin tried to model the best approaches to interpreting the Bible in his many published commentaries on the biblical books. It was as a lecturer on the Bible that Calvin was first employed in Geneva, and he saw his production of commentaries as the very heart of his calling. This was a good thing, because, by most accounts, he was a gifted biblical interpreter and expositor. Calvin, the humanist, approached the Bible believing that tools supplied by what we would call the human sciences (chiefly philology and history) were critically important in getting at its meaning. The text had to be read in its original language and placed in its original context. Sometimes this approach yielded startlingly new understandings of the text; Calvin was not at all timid about breaking with traditional readings of biblical passages. The most important thing, he believed, was to get at the genuine sense of a passage and to avoid forced or "subtle" interpretations that served only to conform the text to one's own theological prejudices. With these convictions, Calvin helped pave the way for modern, historical-critical and literary approaches to biblical study. But since Calvin regarded the Bible not simply with antiquarian interests—for him it was a living document through which God continues to speak—his commentaries dwelled not only on original meanings but also on implications for his own time. The experiences of his contemporaries, especially the harrowing trials of the underground faith communities he addressed, were always an important element in his reflection on the biblical text.

Tool 4: A Guide to Theological Understanding

Of all his productions, Calvin's *Institutes of the Christian Religion* probably had the greatest impact on the development of the spreading

Reformed movement. It was the work of his life, and it largely accounts for his ongoing theological legacy. The short text he published in 1536 was just the beginning of it. He made major revisions and expansions of the book in 1539, 1543, 1550, and 1559. In its final form, the work had grown from the initial six chapters to a total of eighty chapters in four books! The Latin version of the *Institutes* quickly became the most widely used theological textbook for Reformed students, while the many vernacular translations spread Calvin's influence among a lay audience that extended far beyond Geneva. So significant was the impact of this text, so compelling and persuasive were its arguments and presentation of the Reformed theology, that the first appearance of the text in French (in 1541) almost single-handedly precipitated the campaign of official censorship of "heretical" books by the Sorbonne and the Parlement of Paris in 1542.

The message of the *Institutes* is as complex as Calvin's enigmatic personality and as rich and many-layered as the whole of his theology. It is an expression of his own reading of the Christian faith. And so it reflects the particularities and idiosyncrasies of this sixteenth-century life, the perspective of the French humanist and the Genevan reformer of the church who looked out from Geneva's walls with a sense of responsibility for the destiny of the whole of his world.

Let us look more closely at the basic elements of this message Calvin offered to that world.

Chapter Three

Orienting Theology

How Calvin's Theology Is Organized

When Calvin first set out to write a summary of what Christians believe, he took for a model the order of topics Martin Luther used for his *Small Catechism*: the Law (or Ten Commandments), the Lord's Prayer, the Sacraments, and Christian Duties. Never entirely satisfied with this arrangement, Calvin made changes with each new version of his *Institutes of the Christian Religion* until he finally hit on a way of organizing his theology that (he thought) made perfect sense. It went like this:

1. The Knowledge of God the Creator
2. The Knowledge of God the Redeemer in Christ, First Disclosed to the Fathers under the Law, and Then to Us in the Gospel
3. The Way in Which We Receive the Grace of Christ: What Benefits Come to Us from It, and What Effects Follow
4. The External Means or Aids by Which God Invites Us into the Society of Christ and Holds Us Therein

These were the titles Calvin gave to the four "books" of the 1559 edition of the *Institutes*.

What is significant about this arrangement? Not all of Calvin's interpreters agree on an answer to that question. Did Calvin want to follow the order of the Apostles' Creed, which treats God the Father, Jesus Christ, the Holy Spirit, and the church (in that order)? Or did he divide up his text according to an idea of two kinds of knowledge of

God—the knowledge of God as Creator and the knowledge of God as Redeemer? Whichever answer we choose (or even if we come up with another answer), it seems clear that Calvin did want to highlight the word "knowledge." For Calvin, knowledge was not equivalent to reason. When he used the word, he had in mind the heart as much as the head. But he certainly wanted to explore how it is that human beings are aware of God, how they are related to God, and how God works to change the character of that relationship and to guide them through life to their ultimate destiny. His theology is an attempt to tell that story.

In looking at the story as Calvin presents it, we will follow the order of topics he devised. First, however, we need to look at what he put under the heading of theology.

The First Book: How We Know God as Our Creator

What Theology Is and What It Is Not

Calvin seems not to have called himself a theologian. Perhaps he associated the term with the professional scholastic university teachers he called "Sophists." For them, Calvin suggested, theology was a process of "cold" and "arid" reasoning. Cool, detached, and objective, it lacked passion. It had no heat. For Calvin, theology had to be hot, that is, it had to engage the emotions—the heart and the soul. If theology was idle speculation, an exercise of indulging our curiosity, then busy people who want to know about life's vital questions should throw it out! (Curiosity was not an attribute to be encouraged, in Calvin's view. He cites approvingly the answer to the old question about what God was doing before the creation of the world: God was building hell for curious persons.)

Theology has to do with the vital questions, questions that cut to the center of our existence. It looks for knowledge, not mere information. It seeks wisdom, not facts (since many facts elude our limited human understanding). There is, in the enterprise of theology, a quest for truth. But theology is not about taming mystery or reducing it to a set of logical propositions. It is, instead, a practical search for a way of speaking about the fundamental questions of our life.

So when Calvin begins his reflections on a Christian theological orientation, he begins with the broadest of vital questions—Who is God? Who am I?—what he calls the knowledge of God and of ourselves. Like reflection on chickens and eggs, thinking about what we know of God and ourselves involves us in a quandary. Which comes first? With which should we begin? It is impossible to decide. On one hand, it seems that we would need to have an understanding of who we are before we set about to contemplate more lofty matters. But we cannot think about ourselves without thinking about where we have come from, about the one who has created us, the one in whom we live and move and have our being (Acts 17:28). On the other hand, we don't have a clear vision of ourselves unless we look at the one who is our Creator. Rather than choosing one or the other as a starting point, Calvin says we need to look at both. We need to consider the *relation* of God and ourselves. And that will mean moving back and forth between reflection on who God is and who we human beings are, in the context of this relation.

It is worth noting one of the things Calvin refuses to do as he begins the process of theological reflection. He does not pause to prove God's existence. This is because Calvin did not think that theological reflection had to do with laying a rational basis for faith or belief. Instead, theology assumed faith. Like the eleventh-century theologian Anselm of Canterbury (1033–1109), theology for Calvin was "faith seeking understanding." He felt that all people of faith (and, in fact, all people *period*) knew there was a God. It would be a waste of valuable time to engage in proofs to tell honest people what they already knew, proofs that, in any case, would not convince the skeptical (since they were willfully dishonest). On the other hand, the discourse of theology is not *only* for persons who already possess a firm faith. Theology should aim to persuade skeptics—and Calvin uses his rhetorical gifts to accomplish this—but it won't be persuasive if it tries to build a deductive, rationalistic, or speculative system.

A Primal and Natural Awareness

So Calvin begins by assuming God's existence, assuming that we are related to God as our creator, and assuming that somewhere, deep within us, we know or are aware of God. All we have to do is look at ourselves, Calvin says, and we can see the marvels of God's handiwork. Look at the incredible creation that is a human being: the body with its perfect balance, the intricacies of its anatomy and physiology, its physical beauty. Here, surely, are "enough miracles to occupy our minds." The human soul, mind, or consciousness, with its imagination, intelligence, and creativity, shows "unfailing signs of divinity." And what of the world beyond ourselves? The wonders of nature: the stars in the night sky following their courses, the majesty of Niagara Falls, the grandeur of the Grand Canyon (alright, alright, Calvin didn't know about those last two, but he did have the Alps!). Only the most insensitive of souls can contemplate the universe and fail to experience the wisdom, power, and goodness of the Creator. Nature is, according to Calvin, a theater of God's glory, "crammed with innumerable miracles." It is a visible image of the invisible God. A pious person can even say that nature *is* God, so clearly does the natural world show God to us. But since, in fact, God is the creative power at work in and over nature, it is better not to confuse the Creator with the creation.

There is something in us, then, that we can call the natural knowledge of God. It is there in us, and we have access to it when we contemplate ourselves and the world. Another way of talking about this is to say that all human beings have a "seed of religion." History and anthropology show us that humans are religious beings. That is, they not only have an awareness of God, they fashion ways of responding to God—through worship and representations of deity. Unfortunately, in Calvin's view, these are inevitably gross distortions of true religion. Because instead of being content to respond genuinely to God, humans construct their own, distorted images of the divine. They make and worship idols, their own projections, as fetishes to harness sacred power for their own use. The human mind, according to Calvin, is a "perpetual factory of idols." We prefer, that is, to worship our fabricated and domesticated gods than to respond to the living God. And we are, he says, highly adept at creating these gods; our lives are filled with a profusion of tangible substitutes for the intangible God. The seed of religion takes root in us and grows into a malformed plant that gives bitter fruit.

Idols and Images

Like the early Christians, Calvin associated this penchant toward idolatry with pagan religion. But he believed that it could be found in every historical instance of religion—even Christianity. Religious practice in his own time and place was full of idolatry, Calvin said. It was especially evident in the tendency to equate God's power with material things. People would travel great distances to come to a place that held a piece of the cross on which Jesus was crucified, a drop of the Virgin Mary's milk, or an image or the remains of a great saint. They believed that sacred power emanated from these relics and that venerating them was a worthy act. Calvin wrote a scathing attack on popular devotion to relics, pointing out how collectors of holy objects fooled the common people: "St Anne, the mother of the Blessed Virgin, has a whole body at Apt in Provence, and another at Notre-Dame-de-l'Ile in Lyon. She has one head at Trier, a second at Düren in Jülich, and a third in a town named after her in Thuringia. I shall not speak of her other relics shown in more than a hundred different places." He recalled that as a small boy he himself had kissed one of these relics at an abbey near Noyon on a day set aside to honor Saint Anne's remains.[3]

Kissing or showing honor to a saint's relics might seem to be innocent enough. Catholic piety was, at the time, and in important ways continues to be, strongly sacramental, focusing on physical embodiments of the sacred in the midst of life. But to Calvin, this piety violated the first two of the Ten Commandments ("You shall have no other gods before me" and "You shall not make for yourself an idol, whether in the form of anything that is in heaven above, or that is on the earth beneath, or that is in the water under the earth. You shall not bow down to them or worship them" [Exod. 20:3–5]). The official theology of the church distinguished between the kind of veneration offered to saints and the worship and service given to God alone. But Calvin insisted that this was a false distinction, given human psychology and our tendency to worship what is tangible and visible as opposed to the spiritual worship we owe to the invisible God. With Luther, Calvin insisted that whatever a person bowed down to and served, whatever her heart clung to, became her God. And to offer religious veneration to a saint's image carved in wood or to the remains of human flesh was simple idol worship. The concern over idolatry led Calvin and others in the Reformed movement to reject visual depictions of God, Jesus, or any of the saints. Paintings, drawings, or sculptures of this kind would only encourage the popular inclination to fixate on the material as opposed to the spiritual.

Did the Bible's prohibition against rendering God in a visual way and worshiping "wood and stone" (Ezek. 20:32) mean that Christians would need to reject all art? Calvin did not think that was necessary. After all, he lived in the age of the Renaissance, with its enthusiastic revival of classical art forms. He approved of the many gifts of artistic expression, including music and the visual arts, as manifestations of God's goodness to human beings and a source of instruction and delight. But Calvin saw a problem when these arts found their way into worship space. Take, for example, a work of art produced when Calvin was an infant and one of the most famous paintings of the sixteenth century, *The Creation of Adam* by the Italian master Michelangelo (1474–1564). In this painting, one of the scenes decorating the ceiling of the Sistine Chapel in Rome, we see a semi-recumbent Adam with left arm extended, his finger almost touching the finger of God, whose arm reaches out toward the newly formed man. God, like his creature, has human form, an older, male figure, accompanied by angelic beings and seemingly free from the gravitational force that keeps Adam lying down. This is one of the iconic Western portrayals of God, with the Creator imaged as an old but still vigorous and muscular man, with a long white beard and flowing white hair. It's a beautiful and touching depiction of an event that Michelangelo surely realized did not conform exactly to his imaginative depiction. No one knows what creation looked like. So what harm is there in allowing the artist's imagination to use its gifts to represent the emotional meaning of a Bible story?

The problem, according to Calvin, is that once you've looked at this picture, a certain damage has been done. It has conveyed to you a mental image of God as physically embodied, on a par with his creature, as a sort of ideal older male figure with all the parts (presumably) that any human male has, sharing the fair complexion of this version of Adam, and so on. In other words, instead of receiving what God discloses to us about who God is, you have allowed a highly particular fashioning of God to come into your consciousness. And once there, Calvin believed, this image and others like it tend to fix our idea of God in distorting ways. A limited, human, material conception of the divine takes root and crowds out the biblical idea of a vast, unlimited, spiritual, and invisible God who is far beyond our ability to capture in any representation. And that fixing of God is a component of idolatry. It is one thing to encounter such an image in a museum. But Calvin thought that to bring it into the space of prayer introduces a constant danger to human beings who need lots of help to resist temptations to domesticate God.

The attack on images—Calvin's iconoclasm—is important because it points to the critical spirit that became a central part of his legacy. Calvin criticized freely the religious ideas and practices of his day. And he did so in order to distinguish truth from error. Errors had become confused with truth simply because they carried with them the weight of custom and tradition. The effort to expose error and distinguish the living God from false and idolatrous depictions became a hallmark of Calvinism and of a number of other related movements in the modern world.

Corrective Lenses

Let's come back to how we know God. We know God through our encounter with the world God has created, but we make a mess of that knowledge. We look out on the spectacle of God's glory in nature and we don't see it properly. Through our misuse of the natural knowledge of God, all those evidences of God's goodness have become a blur to us. We need some sort of means of correcting our faulty vision. And, fortunately for us, Calvin says, we have such a means! God accommodates our inability to see by providing us a pair of eyeglasses in God's word.

What is God's word? It is the way God has spoken to humanity from Adam and Eve on; through Abraham, through Moses, through prophets and apostles, God communicates to us. And we have that word, in the present, in the form of Scripture. Scripture, then, is the way we come to know God. There are other sources for the knowledge of God. But only with the aid of the insight Scripture gives can we make sense of those other sources.

A Question of Authority

Calvin, along with Luther and other contemporary Protestant reformers, wanted to establish a central place for the Bible in theological reflection. Scripture, as compared to the authority of the pope and the traditional teachings of the church, was paramount. But to some Catholic opponents, pitting the authority of Scripture against the church made no sense. As Johann Eck, an early critic of Luther, said, "The church is older than Scripture, for when the Apostles began to preach, there was no written Gospel, no letter of Paul, and yet there was the church dedicated by Christ's blood." Moreover, "Scripture is not authentic without the church's authority." Who determined which books were to be included in the canon of Scripture? The church. And what entity instructs Christians in the meaning of Scripture? Clearly, it is the church. So, Catholics argued, the church is the first and more basic authority.[4]

Against these claims, Calvin argued that to place the church above Scripture is to try to put human authority over the authority of God. In fact, the church is not older than Scripture. Scripture is simply the written word of God. And the word of God is as old as God's speaking to humanity. How did the church come to be? Through the calling of God in God's word and the preaching of prophets and apostles who were God's mouthpiece. And, although it may seem to be the case that the church decided arbitrarily which books would be included and which would be left out of the Bible, in fact decisions about the biblical canon were always made on the basis of the authority these books had *already* come to possess in the community of the faithful. It was God's word that established that authority, not the decision of human beings. And so, says Calvin, the authority of Scripture must be recognized as the higher authority. It is the means through which we hear the very voice of God.

But how do we know God speaks in Scripture? We know it because we experience God speaking in Scripture. That is, we become certain that Scripture is God's word to us when God's Spirit testifies to us, or confirms to us, that this is God's word. Here Calvin's reasoning seems to be circular, but the circularity is not unintentional. To try to establish the authority of the Bible by adducing proofs or by appealing to some criteria outside of God's word to us would be to create another authority higher than Scripture, an authority on which we would then have to depend for trusting that we hear God when we read the Bible. But Scripture doesn't need any external proof. "The proof of the pudding is in the eating," goes the old saying. And much the same could be said for Scripture. There are no proofs of Scripture's authenticity higher or more effective than the internal conviction of one who has heard God speaking to her through the biblical word.

But doesn't God speak to people in other ways, outside of the Bible? What about the Holy Spirit? Calvin does believe God speaks through the Holy Spirit. The Spirit, however, is the "author" of Scripture. As an author, the Spirit speaks consistently—not one way in the book and another way when whispering in our ears. Instead of thinking of the Holy Spirit as speaking independently of the Bible, says Calvin, we should recognize that God's word is the instrument God has chosen through which to teach us. Calvin concedes that not everyone sees the light when they read the Bible. This is because it is only when the Spirit illumines us in our reading of the Bible and changes the dead letter on the page to a word of life that we discover God's word to us. And so, while he placed a great deal of emphasis on the text of the Bible as the word of God, Calvin also recognized that the Spirit must work upon readers and the believing community to make the word a life-giving power in their own time and place.

Calvin thinks of God—in the person of the Holy Spirit—as the author of Scripture. When he says this, he doesn't mean to suggest that the Bible has no human authors or that the function of human authors (e.g., Moses,

Jeremiah, Matthew, Paul) was simply to write down words dictated by the Spirit. It would be hard to read Jeremiah or Paul and fail to recognize that profoundly human personalities are present in their writings. No, to say God is the author of Scripture means that God is the one who speaks a message in and through the words of Jeremiah and Paul.

Going to School

Calvin was a teacher, and if those who studied with him can be believed, he was a good one. His humanist training in rhetoric prepared him to use language effectively to communicate ideas to his students and to lead them, persuasively, toward the truth. It is not surprising then that Calvin depicts God as a teacher and as a master of rhetoric. A good rhetorician knows his audience. He knows their language. He knows what images will resonate with them. He aims precisely at their level of comprehension. He puts the message, in other words, into just the right medium so that it has the desired effect on his audience.

Scripture, according to Calvin, is like God's schoolroom. It is the environment within which we learn of God and of ourselves. It is not a collection of facts, an assortment of data about God. It is the medium in which we encounter God's message to us. When we turn to examine that medium, Calvin says, we discover that God, the master rhetorician, *accommodates* human understanding in it.

What does that mean?

Calvin thought that educated readers of the Bible in his time, who came to the text expecting its eloquence to reflect the literary values of the Renaissance, would be disappointed. The Bible is not, in his view, sophisticated philosophical discourse. Its stories, poems, chronicles, legal codes, and letters reflect the world and worldviews out of which these particular texts emerged. According to Calvin, God made use of the idioms of ancient language and culture and in so doing "stooped down" to the level of the audience, accommodating their limited ability in order to communicate with them. You might say (and Calvin does say) that Scripture is God's baby talk. Just as adults will alter their speech when talking to a baby in order to suit the infant's capacity to understand, God puts things in terms chosen to suit the capacity of the hearers of the biblical text. We won't be surprised then to find ancient conceptions of the cosmos in texts of the Old Testament. We shouldn't be shocked to find God walking around in the garden of Eden in Genesis 3. And we shouldn't suppose that this proves that God has feet.

A significant consequence of this idea, when it comes to interpreting the Bible, is that it makes it possible for the reader of Scripture to attend to the very human aspect of the text (the way it reflects characteristics of language, thought forms, and cultural understandings that are historically particular and possibly different from our own) even as she takes the Bible seriously as God's word. The Bible is not some sort of unmediated divine discourse (whatever that might be: perhaps how God talks to himself when he's shaving, or her interior monologue as she's on the Stairmaster). It is a means of communication that uses the means available in, and appropriate to, particular times and places. And so the biblical interpreter is justified in using scientific tools (linguistics, philology, history, anthropology) in studying these very human aspects of the Bible.

The Creator Revealed

I have spent some time dealing in depth with Calvin's understanding of the Bible and its authority because for Calvin this was a critical piece of his theological understanding. All of what we have to say theologically, about God and ourselves, depends upon how we interpret the Bible.

Now that Calvin has established his view of the Bible's authority he can turn to look at what we learn there about the Creator and the creation. We have already seen that the Creator has to be distinguished from the many idols humans create. But who is that masked man? According to Calvin, not a man at all. (But, given the description that follows, we might be tempted to say *three* men—or perhaps two men and a bird.)

We find, that is, that Scripture shows us God as eternal spirit and as *one* ("Hear, O Israel: the LORD our God is one." [Deut. 6:4 KJV]). But we also find God to be *three*: Father, Son or Word, and Holy Spirit. Although the Bible doesn't give us in any direct way the terms to describe "oneness" alongside "threeness" or to make sense of this apparent contradiction, Calvin claims that the traditional, and orthodox, doctrine of the Trinity—speaking of one divine essence and three divine persons—is the right way of explaining what Scripture teaches. All three persons are, together, one God. Each is eternal. And each represents a peculiar function of God (which we will deal with in due course), although all together are active in each function.

Affirming a Trinitarian view of God is certainly nothing new. But since the Bible itself doesn't really have such a doctrine, and Calvin maintained that all doctrine should be derived from the Bible, it was significant that Calvin chose to make this affirmation. Some of those involved in the reformation movements had suggested that the doctrine of the Trinity—or, at any rate, some of the traditional terms used to express the idea—should be abandoned. One of the most radical critics of Trinitarian understandings, Michael Servetus, played an important role in Calvin's thinking about the importance of the traditional teaching. We will come back to Servetus and his encounters with Calvin in the next chapter.

A Good Creation and Its Creatures

It is this God, whom we discover to be a Trinity, who is the source of all things. God created the world and "it was very good"—or so the self-congratulatory Creator of the first chapter of Genesis seems to have thought. Calvin agrees that creation is good, very good. This creation includes, in his view, spiritual beings: angels and, yes, fallen angels—including a devil. Although that last fact might seem to call into question the claim of goodness, Calvin insists that it does not. God is in control of all things—even the devil, who can do nothing apart from God's willing. But these spiritual beings are not the center of creation and the focus of God's attention. That honor belongs to human beings.

In humanity we find, says Calvin, "the most noble and excellent specimen of the righteousness, wisdom, and goodness of God." Humans, at the center of this very good creation, are very good themselves. And they are special. As Genesis 1:26 puts it, they are created in the image and likeness of God—which is to say that, apart from all other creatures, they are created by God in such a way as to enjoy a special relationship with God. Biblical testimony of this divine image shows us that there was no original fault in the first humans. They were created with free will—the freedom to choose to do what is good. In all aspects of created human nature, says Calvin, we see mind-boggling reflections of God's glory. It seems Calvin can't say enough good things about humanity as created by God.

This rhapsodizing on human goodness may come as a surprise to those who associate Calvin with a pessimistic view of human nature. (Of course, we should wait to see what he is going to say next!) In some ways, his painting in such vivid colors "the perfect excellence of human nature" sets up a stark contrast with our nature as we experience it *now* (after a certain fall). But that is not all Calvin is doing. He is also pointing us toward God's goodness. God cares for humans. And, as we look at all the evidence of the conditions of our first creation, we see wonderful testimonies to God's wise care and affection for the human creature.

God's Providence

When we reflect on God's relation to the world, it is not enough to speak of God as Creator of the world. That way of speaking could lead us to conclude that the world was set in motion by God, constructed and wound up as a clockmaker would a clock, and then left to function on its own. Then we would have a view of God as distant from us and removed from everything that happens in our world. That would not be Calvin's God; nor would a spectator God, gazing down from the heavens to see what's going to happen next. The Creator Scripture points to is also the one who continually governs and preserves the universe.

But what sort of governing? Using the analogy of recent U.S. presidents, is God mainly concerned with the big picture, leaving the minutiae of governing to others—say, like a Reagan or the younger Bush? Or is God more of a micromanager, unable to resist administrative details, on the order of Carter or Clinton? Calvin's description of God leans toward the model of the recent Democrats. Not only does God rule the world by universal laws of nature, "he sustains, nourishes, and cares for everything he has made, even to the least sparrow." God's hands are in everything.

When Calvin speaks of God's providence, he has in mind this conception of God's intimate involvement in the world. And our experience of God's providence leads us to think of God's power. God's involvement with the world is dynamic and powerful to the extent that "nothing takes place without God's deliberation." The view of God's relation to the world that Calvin finds in the Bible suggests that we make a mistake when we try to encourage someone by wishing them "good luck." There is no such thing as luck, good or bad, since every eventuality is a consequence of God's willing and working. It may seem that we are at the mercy of fortune or chance, but in fact God is active in and through everything in every moment.

To some critics, that view smacks of what they call fatalism, or a deterministic view of the world. The ancient Greek and Roman Stoics who first expressed this view denied that anyone possessed freedom. Both for God and for humans, what they do is a consequence of an impersonal power called fate. But Calvin claimed that the biblical view is different from the view of determinism. God is free, says Calvin. And so are humans. Even though God is active in everything that occurs, including everything I do, I remain free in my choices. That is, I experience my choices and acts as free and not constrained. They come as the consequence of what I will. And yet, it is true at the same time that God's willing and acting are effective in and through the free wills of conscious agents (like me and all humans) as well as through the course of natural events (like rain showers, lunar eclipses, or the movement of asteroids). Calvin's point is that this understanding of God's providence doesn't reduce us to the status of automatons or marionettes whose strings are pulled by God.

Even with this assertion of freedom, the idea that "God causes everything" makes some people uncomfortable because not everything that happens in the world is something we think a good God ought to be given credit for. Whether we have in mind catastrophic natural events—tsunamis, tornadoes, plagues—or the horrible things that happen because of what we humans do (and in an age of global warming, we could include natural disasters in this category too), we have to face a troubling question: How can the presence of things in creation that cause enormous suffering be reconciled with the view that God is good? If God "does everything," how can we avoid saying that God is the one who introduces evil into the world?

The simple answer is that we can't. God is active in every human act and every natural event. And yet it would be wrong for us, Calvin thinks, to conceive of God as responsible for evil in the way we ordinarily talk about moral culpability. Why is that? Because when we assess the morality of an act we look at a number of factors, including the *intention* of the one who acts and the *outcome* of the act. We know, says Calvin, that when humans act in hurtful ways they frequently intend harm, and they frequently cause it. But in all those instances of events that cause suffering, God works to bring outcomes that are, ultimately—and from God's point of view—good. Our limited vantage point does not always allow us to assess this. We cannot see anything like ultimate outcomes. And so the best we can do is to trust that God is acting for good, even as suffering is occurring.

That answer will not satisfy those who cannot abide a picture of God who causes suffering. But it is worth noting that whenever Calvin referred to this understanding of divine providence his language reflected enormous compassion. In a moment of crisis for members of the underground Reformed community of Paris in 1557, he wrote encouraging words to those affected by the threat of violent death, referring to the words of Psalm 56: "Do not doubt that God has an eye on you.... Even though he might not stretch out his hand to succor us as soon as we would wish, let us never give up on the conviction that the hairs of our head are numbered, and that if he sometimes allows the blood of his people to be shed, yet he never fails to gather up their precious tears." For Calvin, the idea of God's providence was a great comfort, especially to those who were at the mercy of events and forces beyond their control. For those enduring harsh persecution, the conviction that God was in control, that God offered "shelter in the shadow of his wings," and that goodness and justice would finally prevail was the basis for the hope that sustained them.[5]

This is a fitting note on which to conclude our discussion of the first major section of Calvin's theological portrait. In this understanding of providence we find a characteristic feature of the Calvinist outlook: We need to rely, absolutely, on God. Book 1 of the *Institutes* is dedicated to that message, and it lays a foundation for its development in the books to follow. Knowledge of God cannot be had by human striving. It comes only when we receive God as God shows God's self to us. We cannot capture God in our images. We must receive the images—the word—that God makes available to us. And we can and should trust our lives, and the course of history, to no power but the power of God.

The Second Book: How We Know God as Our Redeemer

Just as in the first book of the *Institutes*, where "The Knowledge of God the Creator" leads us to talk as well about who human beings are as creatures of God, when Calvin turns to examine how we know God as our Redeemer, he has to deal with who we know ourselves to be, namely, persons in need of redemption.

Sin and Its Source

If somewhere at the heart of the Calvinist view of the world is the notion that human beings must depend completely on God, then Calvin's doctrine of sin is a crucial part of achieving that view. Calvin says, "We cannot seriously aspire to God until we have begun to be displeased with ourselves."

Being displeased with oneself is not a goal many aspire to these days. Self-esteem is something that, of course, everyone needs, and we see disastrous consequences when a person lacks a basic sense of his or her worth. But there are a variety of ways of achieving a sense of self-worth. Calvin believed that there are some mistaken ways. And the most dangerous of these, in his view, are those that misjudge our capacity for goodness or for moral improvement. In Calvin's time there were plenty of Renaissance depictions of "man" that were extremely flattering to men (especially the wealthy Renaissance patrons who commissioned these portrayals). We might think of more recent trends that echo this optimistic mentality: all the various "healthy-minded" philosophies of self-improvement that can be sampled in the self-help section of your local bookstore. But Calvin's complaint was that these cheery portraits had to overlook a good deal about human nature, especially the evil of which it is capable. The cost of making one feel good about oneself was overlooking the real deficiencies, in fact the fatal flaw, in the self. And without attending to the disease afflicting human nature, thought Calvin, there is no hope for finding the right cure.

That is one reason why Calvin attends so carefully to sin and why he depicts it in such extravagant terms. Calvin's view of human sin, or human fallenness, is very close to the position Augustine argued against the optimist of his time, Pelagius. When the songwriter Bruce Springsteen portrays characters who are trapped in circumstances not entirely of their own making but for which they share responsibility, he echoes Augustine's view. The lyrics "You're born into this life paying / For the sins of someone else's past," in the song "Adam Raised a Cain," characterize a particular father-son relationship, but they can be applied more broadly to express the idea of original sin Augustine introduced in the early fifth century. That view was that the first parents of humankind, Adam and Eve, although created good and innocent, through their own choice fell into sin. And that fateful fall affected all their posterity (cf. Rom. 5:12).

The sin of the first humans is known as original sin. The tradition derived from Augustine equated the sin of Adam and Eve with pride. But Calvin thought that the essence of sin was not pride but lack of faith or trust in God. It was because they first let go of their trust in God that Adam and Eve then fell into pride, trying to assert their self-sufficiency and their independence from God. This primal sin affected not just these two persons but the whole human race. It did so because of the solidarity of humanity in the first members of the race. Original sin, then, determines the condition of every child born into this world. And so, from our present vantage point, we can say that human nature, although created good, is no longer quite so good. Yes, we possess the image of God in which human beings were first created. But it is not what it used to be. Now it is "a horrible deformity." We can see glimpses of what God intended for us when we look at who we are, but only *very* fleeting ones. And they give us no ground for encouragement.

All Sin, All the Time!

Calvin is well-known for talking about the effects of sin as "total depravity." Human sin, in his view, creates a condition whose effects are "diffused into all parts of the soul." The "total" in "total depravity" means that there is no part of the human personality that is free from sin and its impact. Why would Calvin want to make such a claim? For one thing, to counter the idea that, somewhere within them, humans have some area of their life that is sin free and that, from that area, they can derive the resources to heal themselves of what ails them. We have no such resources, Calvin says. As his prayer of confession puts it, "We are poor sinners, conceived and born in iniquity and corruption, prone to do evil, incapable of any good, and in our depravity we transgress [God's] holy commandments without end or ceasing."

The consequences of sin are many. They involve our ability to discern certain things, such as God. Sin explains why humans so easily fall into idolatry rather than worshiping the true God. And they involve our will. Calvin claims that sinful human beings have a will (still). But is it a free will? Yes, in a certain sense. It is free in the sense that the choices we make are genuinely *our* choices. No one outside of myself forces me to choose in the way I do. But it is not free in that we cannot choose *not* to sin. Original sin has resulted in a binding (or enslavement) of our will, a bondage to sin. We can choose many things. We can choose *how* we will sin. But we cannot determine to do what is good and succeed in doing what is good.

The claim that human beings lack free will is a controversial one. Luther and Erasmus had carried on a vehement public argument over the issue in 1524–1526. As a humanist, Erasmus wanted to preserve the idea that humans are able, on their own, to respond to God; they can improve morally and they can work to better their societies. Calvin engaged in a brief debate (in 1542–1543) with a Catholic opponent, Albertus Pighius, who feared that an attack on human freedom would compromise both the idea of God's goodness and the Catholic emphasis on the need for us to strive for holiness. For both Luther and Calvin, to speak of humans as free, free to do what is good and capable of moral progress, was simply to indulge in self-flattery. Free will is a fiction, they claimed. The effects of primal human sinfulness are too strong for us to claim the capacity to do good apart from God.

This assertion of the seriousness of sin and its impact sets the stage for the next important scene in Calvin's drama of Christian faith. In that scene appears the Mediator, also known as Jesus Christ. But before the

Mediator can make an entrance, there is a significant prologue introducing him and explaining where he fits in the drama of God's word of redemption.

A Legal Precedent

Jesus Christ, naturally, plays a central role in Calvin's understanding of what Christian religion is all about. In fact, for Calvin, we do not know God properly apart from Christ. But, lest we think that that means that no one knew God properly before the birth of a baby to Mary in Bethlehem, he assures us that God was known—both as Creator and as Redeemer—in earlier times. Sin, the barrier that humans erected between themselves and God, did not prevent God from reaching out to humans. Scripture testifies to God's persistent search for reconciliation with God's creatures. A principal way in which God reached out was through covenants, those agreements in which God offered promises of blessing and faithfulness to ancient Israel. A centerpiece of the covenant-making that is reflected in the Bible is the law.

When Calvin speaks of the law, he has in mind the whole system of religion that was handed down by God, as he believed, to Moses, and that was practiced by the people of the Old Testament. It includes the ceremonial, religious, or cultic portions of the law, as well as the judicial law, but its heart is the moral law, summarized in the Ten Commandments. Calvin followed his close Lutheran friend, Philip Melanchthon, in claiming that the moral law served three uses.

- The first of these uses is *pedagogical*: Like a stern pedagogue of Calvin's time, it knocks sense into those it teaches. It serves as a mirror, Calvin says, showing us who we are—namely, sinners. We fail to do what the law says we should do and succeed in doing what the law says we shouldn't. This was merely an echo of Paul's assertion that "through the law comes the knowledge of sin" (Rom. 3:20). Seeing clearly our sin, with the help of the law, we "dismiss the stupid opinion of [our] own strength" and "flee to God's mercy."
- The second use of the law is *political*. That is, the law works to restrain wrongdoers—persons who would not keep from breaking out into violent and destructive behavior were it not for the threats and punishments the law lays down.
- The third use Calvin calls the *principal* use: The law works to guide faithful persons and to spur them on toward holiness. Unlike the

first two uses, which are intended for people who have not yet experienced the healing, reconciling work God achieves through Jesus Christ, the third use is more positive than punitive. Here the law, like the Word, becomes "a lamp to my feet and a light to my path" (Ps. 119:105); "sweeter also than honey, and drippings of the honeycomb," "rejoicing the heart" (Ps. 19:10, 8).

Calvin's positive assessment of the law contrasts with the positions of some evangelical reformers of his time. Since the Reformation was often characterized as a recovery of "the gospel," which could be understood as the message of the New Testament, might we not say that the law—the collection of all those rules and regulations of the Old Testament (some of which Jesus seemingly challenged)—is not the point and no longer applies? Calvin did not think that a careful reading of the Bible could support such a view. The whole of God's word addressed to us in the Bible still applies to us. However, different parts apply in different ways. The ceremonial law (regulations concerning ritual purity, sacrifice, and so on) no longer applies to the worship of those who have encountered Jesus Christ, as the New Testament explains. The judicial law of Israel and Judah was a political law for a particular time and place. The moral law, however, is universal, and it does apply to us.

Calvin's rejection of a deprecatory treatment of the law might be familiar to us if we tend to place Calvin in a class with the supposedly legalistic, or possibly prudish, villains of traditional Christian histories: the Pharisees, the Puritans, and perhaps the moralizing Victorians. The attraction for him, however, was not legalism so much as it was his love for the text of Scripture.

The law of God is disclosed, first, in a section of the Bible that many Christians had reduced to second-class status. The Old Testament, according to an early critic—the second-century heterodox Christian, Marcion—was not Scripture at all and had no business being in the canon. While the church condemned Marcion, it had no way of interpreting Old Testament texts apart from their direct application to Christ or the Christian faith. If Jesus is the light of the world, as the Gospel of John states, that must mean the people of the Old Testament lived in a time of darkness. Maybe there were some glimmers of light there—after all, there are passages from the Old Testament that New Testament writers later applied to Jesus—but only glimmers, right?

Wrong, Calvin says. He rejects the second-class ranking of the Old Testament. It contains God's promise of salvation addressed to the people of Israel. He believed firmly that that promise points to Christ. And so, in his reading, redemption in Christ is the heart of all Scripture. But that does not mean that we need only pay attention to those parts of the Old Testament that seem to be speaking of the baby who will be born to Mary. Again, the whole of Scripture is the medium for God's word to us: We need to pay attention to the Old Testament because it tells the story of how God reached out to God's people, taught, cajoled, threatened, pleaded, and all the time kept faith with them, having promised to be their God and their Savior. That promise bore fruit in those times, as it led to salvation for the saints of the Old Testament and kept hope alive in trying times. But, Calvin observed, the coming of Jesus witnessed the full realization of the promise.

The Mediator

When Calvin considers who Jesus Christ is (his *person*) he finds that it is hard to separate this from what he does (his *work*). Calvin's favorite title for Jesus Christ—the mediator—expresses this connection between identity and function. Christ is the one who stands in between humanity and God and reconciles us to God.

His reflection on these matters is mostly unoriginal. He generally follows earlier theologians' lines of argument as to why a God-man was necessary to heal the breach between God and human beings that sin created. According to the inherited view, our sin has made a mess of things. Theodor Geisel (better known as Dr. Seuss) captures the seriousness of the situation nicely:

> And this mess is so big
> And so deep and so tall,
> We can not pick it up.
> There is no way at all![6]

There is no way, of course, not only because of the dimensions of the muddle but also because sin has vitiated our own ability to do what is required of us, to pick it up. So, then, what power but God's could clean up the mess we have made of ourselves and our world? But the obligation to clean up the mess, to make amends for the wrongs we humans have done, lies only with us. It makes sense, therefore, that God's *ability* and human *obligation* be joined together in a single individual. And so Jesus Christ comes into human history as the fully divine and fully human mediator between us and God (1 Tim.

2:5). For Calvin, such an arrangement was not, strictly speaking, *necessary*, but we know from Scripture that this is the arrangement God chose.

Jesus is the fully human embodiment of God—God's goodness, righteousness, wisdom, and power to save—in our history. The early Christians debated how one should conceive of Jesus as human and divine, and the majority agreed on some guidelines in the Symbol of Chalcedon of 451. Calvin adopts these guidelines and emphasizes them in the following way:

1. Jesus is the incarnation of the eternal Word of God that the Gospel of John speaks about ("In the beginning was the Word, and the Word was with God, and the Word was God" [John 1:1]). The Word is one of the three persons of the Trinity, and so is fully divine.
2. To say that Jesus is the Word incarnate means more than that he simply appeared to be human; he is genuinely and authentically human ("like us in every way apart from sin" [cf. Heb. 4:15]).
3. And so we can talk about Jesus as having two natures—a human and a divine nature. It would be a mistake
    a. to confuse the two,
    b. to say that one changes into the other,
    c. to divide up Christ into two distinct persons,
    d. or to separate the two natures.
4. Jesus Christ, then, is a single person; and yet within that single person are two distinct natures. Should we lose the distinction, "mixing heaven and earth," we would lose something crucial to who Jesus is.
    a. He is certainly one of us (since otherwise we would not benefit from his earthly presence).
    b. And in him the free transcendence and power of God's Word are present (since otherwise the ability of God to save through him would be in doubt).

The union of God and humanity in a single person is not yet, however, equivalent to the work of reconciling humanity to God. To describe that work, Calvin looks at what Jesus does, under the heading of standard biblical types.

- He is a *prophet*; that is, he is one who taught and teaches people about God and about righteousness.

- He is a *king*; that is, he draws people into a way of life that is pleasing to God and to a community of faith that bends itself to God's will. He elicits from them their ultimate loyalty, sustains them, and generously provides for their spiritual needs.
- Finally, he is a *priest*. Like the priests of ancient Israel, he stands before God as a representative of the people (his sisters and brothers) and offers a sacrifice that is "pleasing to God." Unlike the priests of old, the sacrifice he offers is his own life.

Christ's priestly office points to the crux of Calvin's notion of how Jesus overcomes the alienation of humans from God. The images he uses come directly out of the sacrificial imagery of the Bible and the church's subsequent reflection on those images. According to the sacrificial conception, sin creates antagonism between humans and God. God is "angry" at sin. And humans are (understandably) fearful of the just God whose justice requires death as punishment for sin. The theory of how this state of affairs is overcome involves what is known as vicarious atonement or substitutionary punishment. That is, Jesus becomes the sacrificial victim who stands in the place of sinners, does what they could not do themselves (lives a life of perfect obedience to God), and endures on their behalf the punishment that was rightfully theirs. Because he takes the place of sinners, he frees them from the penalty for their sin and wins redemption for them.

Calvin is aware that this image of an angry God demanding the death of guilty persons, refusing to relax the harsh demands of justice, accepting as a substitute the death of an innocent man, and finally being placated by this act of violence, may appear, at the very least, strange and possibly also at odds with our idea of a good and loving God. Calvin believes that the sacrificial imagery discloses something significant about the way we are reconciled to God. But, he warns, we shouldn't interpret the symbolism too literally.

- First, we need to recognize that, although God's wrath is something sinful human beings *do* experience, God's love is the constant motive that lies behind all God's dealings with us.
- Second, God is not an angry judge, passively awaiting a victim before responding with pleasure at the violent outcome. God, we have to remember, is present in Jesus Christ. And so God is both

the agent of redemption and a participant in the suffering that overcomes our alienation.
- Finally, God is not captive to a system of justice (e.g., sin requires death) that God must serve. God could have chosen another means of healing the breach. But God chose this means: to demonstrate the cost of sin, to show the immensity of God's love for us in God's willingness to enter into the pain that unfaithfulness and alienation beget, and to overcome our sense of horror before a righteous God.

And so the imagery of redemption through sacrifice is not meant to show us God in a vindictive mood but rather God as the persistently faithful Savior reaching out to fallen humanity and furnishing the means of their reconciliation.

Jesus' life, his suffering and death, and his rising again do effect a change. It is not, however (despite certain biblical figures of speech), a change in God or in God's attitude toward us (see e.g., Jonah 3:10 RSV: "God repented of the evil which he had said he would do to them"). It is a change in us and in the way we perceive God. We are able, because of Christ, to know God no longer as an angry and righteous judge but as a loving and generous parent. Jesus shows us the loving face of God.

The Third Book: The Inner Work of Healing

If Calvin were content to stick with the objective "facts" of creation, fall, and redemption, the story could end at the conclusion of Book 2. Christ died and rose for sinners. What's left to tell?

Much, as it turns out. In fact, if we measure according to the number of pages, Calvin is only about a quarter of the way through his tale. What does that tell us about Calvin's theology? It tells us that he is concerned not simply with objective facts but with the inner experience of one who is on the receiving end of God's work of love and healing. And so in Book 3 he turns to a description of that experience.

Unio Mystica: *The Work of the Holy Spirit*

The story up to this point has covered the condition afflicting humanity. It has identified the remedy. Now we see how the remedy is administered. The book's title outlines the topic: "The Way in Which We

Receive the Grace of Christ." Calvin focuses in on the burden of this section by claiming that "as long as Christ remains outside of us and we are separated from him, all that he has suffered and done for the salvation of the human race remains useless and of no value to us." The point, then, is to show how Christ "become[s] ours and . . . dwell[s] within us." Calvin will refer to this as a mystical union (*unio mystica*) of believers with Christ.

Calvin is seldom confused with the mystics in the Christian tradition, those who emphasized the possibility of achieving a union with God in which the great distance between humanity and the divine is overcome. And yet Calvin echoes some of their language and emphases, especially the language and ideas of the twelfth-century theologian and mystic Bernard of Clairvaux (1090–1153). He stresses an intimate relationship between Christ and human beings. The images are frequently physical: We partake of (or consume) Christ, we are engrafted into Christ, Christ is poured into us. The point is, without Christ we are lost; but when we are joined to him, we receive all that Christ has (righteousness, goodness, abundant life).

But how does such a union come about? Only, says Calvin, through the work of the Holy Spirit. Up until this point, the Holy Spirit has played a fairly minor part in Calvin's treatment. The Spirit is important, of course, in understanding what Calvin believes about the Bible and how we read and interpret it. But now the Spirit makes more than just a cameo appearance. As Calvin prepares to introduce us to the many facets of the life Christians live in communion with their God, the Spirit plays a major role.

Faith: The Tie That Binds

The Holy Spirit binds us to Christ, says Calvin, by faith. Faith is a gift, given to us by the Spirit. And the Spirit uses our faith as the glue, so to speak, of a mystical union with Christ. So faith is vitally important in Calvin's theology. We would expect that, given that Calvin was influenced by Martin Luther, the reformer who placed justification by faith at the heart of what it means to be Christian. But what does Calvin understand faith to be?

There is no single, standard definition of faith in the Christian tradition. But there are a number of options. Faith can be thought of as belief—believing certain things to be true, such as that God exists or that Jesus is the Son of God—that is, it may have to do primarily with what we know or understand. On the other hand, faith can be treated as not at all dependent on understanding. Perhaps it is enough to want to believe the truth, even if I'm a bit fuzzy on what the truth is exactly. (This is what the church called "implicit faith"—the desire to believe what God reveals and the church teaches.) Faith also can be thought of as something that people have or achieve through great struggle—a spiritual commodity whose possessors we admire. ("She has so much faith!") Or, by contrast, we can think of it as an experience that grasps us, and so not something we would think to claim credit for.

Calvin considers these and some other options before settling on his own definition of faith. It is "a firm and certain knowledge of God's benevolence towards us, founded upon the truth of the freely-given promise in Christ, both revealed to our minds and sealed upon our hearts through the Holy Spirit." Calvin is making several claims about faith in this definition, all of which point to very important aspects of his theology.

- First, faith is personal. It has to do with the individual and her relationship to God. It cannot be had by osmosis. It cannot be borrowed from a friend or associate. It cannot be transferred to us by the church.
- Second, faith is certainly not something that we can claim to have achieved ourselves, since it is the Holy Spirit's gift. Calvin thinks of faith less as a spiritual power or activity than as the vessel of awareness and conviction within us that makes it possible to hold on to God's promise of healing and forgiveness.
- Third, faith has to do with knowledge. But knowledge, for Calvin, is not solely intellectual. It involves the mind—we need to understand certain things (such as who Jesus Christ is and what he has done) in order to have the experience of faith. But it also involves the human affections (it is "sealed upon our hearts"). Precisely for this reason faith cannot be reduced to our assent to certain truths; it involves a fundamental awakening and transformation of life. ("Even the demons believe—and shudder" [Jas. 2:19]; but that sort of "believing" is not genuine faith.) The knowledge that faith entails, in other words, is not like the kind of knowledge one absorbs when reading the stock market report. It is a knowledge that makes a fundamental difference in our perception of self, of God, and of our world, and it changes our way of living in relation to all of these.

Faith makes a difference because it is our grasping onto and our being grasped by God's grace. "Grace" is the word Christians use to describe the unmerited favor God bestows upon humanity. We are "justified by [God's] grace as a gift," said the apostle Paul (Rom. 3:24); and Augustine, reading Paul, made this the centerpiece of his argument against Pelagius that we cannot achieve our own salvation but can receive it only through what God does for us. In God's word, God promises us salvation in Christ, says Calvin. This is the gracious promise that faith apprehends. Faith, then, enables us to accept God's acceptance of us, in Christ. It is the inner conviction that God's promise of salvation is trustworthy and that it applies to me.

We can better sense what faith meant for Calvin, in his context, if we consider its opposite—fear. According to many historians, Calvin lived in an age of fear. This was partly a result of the views of human salvation that were preached to the people and the church practices intended to get Christians into heaven. Salvation was not easily gained. It involved a lifetime of struggling against the lingering effects of original sin and making amends for the daily sins most people found it hard to avoid committing. The sacraments of the church were intended to help in this long process. But it was a process; one was always a pilgrim in this world and never quite sure whether one had done enough to merit the reward of heaven. Should a person die with sins unatoned, he could expect a far less comfortable destination: the interminable pain of hell or the temporary, but usually still very long, suffering in purgatory. The religion that plotted the path to salvation through measuring the balance of sin against works of merit involved for its practitioners a lot of anxiety, anguish, even terror as they weighed who they were against the demands of a righteous God.

Calvin's outlook is based on the rejection of that religion. Faith strives against the fear we feel when we look at who we are and measure ourselves against who we ought to be but cannot be. We are justified, or saved, by this faith.

Faith's Effects: Justification and Sanctification

Calvin argued that the Holy Spirit's gift of faith and union with Christ involves two consequences for believers—regeneration and justification. Christian reflection on justification had always centered on the question of how sinful human beings could be made "just," or acceptable to stand before God. Calvin, agreeing with Luther (and his friend Melanchthon), held that we are not justified by anything we do, by proving our moral or spiritual fitness. Instead, we are justified by God's grace working through faith. Faith binds us to Christ. That binding does not lead to an immediate and intrinsic righteousness in us, as though we suddenly became entirely holy and pure people. We do not. But we are forgiven our sins. And, Calvin says, our incorporation into Christ involves a real sharing in all his benefits, including his righteousness. The righteousness that belongs to Jesus, then, is what justifies, or saves, us. We are acceptable to God not because we have become good people but because we are, as Calvin says, "clothed" in the goodness or righteousness of Christ.

But isn't something important left out here? Aren't religious people supposed to be good? Calvin agrees; yes, of course we need to be good. But we shouldn't confuse the whole question of justification by trying to fit into it the requirement that we be good before God can accept us. The whole message of the Bible (and certainly of Paul's letters), Calvin thinks, is that God accepts us in spite of who we are.

But goodness has its place. That place is not in justification but in sanctification or regeneration. Regeneration can be explained this way. God accepts us in spite of who we are. Through our faith in Christ, God chooses to view us as good or righteous, even though we are not quite that. But God wants us to be good. And so God, in the form of the Holy Spirit, works on us. As we are united with Christ and share his benefits, the Spirit works to make us actually "look" more like Christ (or as Calvin puts it, the Spirit "conforms us to the image of Christ" [cf. Rom. 8:29]). In the case of most of us, that is a difficult assignment. What is required is what we might think of as spiritual and moral reconstructive surgery. Nastiness has to be chiseled away. Goodness and beauty have to be reconstituted out of the "ruin of our nature." Calvin, using more traditional language, calls this "mortification of the flesh" (the doing away of the sinful nature in us) and "vivification of the Spirit" (bringing to life a "new" creation [Rom. 6:4; 2 Cor. 5:17]). The Spirit's work upon us is what we experience as repentance: turning our backs on an old way of life (defined in terms of our sin) and turning to a new life (defined in terms of our relation with Christ). Repentance, and the sanctifying or regenerating work of the Spirit, is a lifelong task. And so, in this life, we don't experience perfection. But we can expect to see progress, Calvin says, and that progress aims toward the restoration of the image of God, which turns out also to be the image of Christ—the condition of freedom and righteousness in which we were originally created.

The life of Christian faith, then, is marked by two (related but distinct) experiences: the experience of being forgiven and accepted by God in spite of our very real failings and the experience of being changed, dealing with our failings, and determining to be true disciples of Christ. "If any want to become my followers, let them deny themselves and take up their cross and follow me" (Matt. 16:24). This brief statement, in which Jesus laid out the terms of discipleship, becomes for Calvin a guide to the task of living out a life that witnesses to Christ's influence upon us. At its heart is self-denial, recognizing that "we are not our own" but belong to God. In other words, Christians do not seek to establish their independence from God. They do not seek to lift themselves above their sisters and brothers. Instead, they seek in all things what is God's will and the good of their neighbor. They bear up under life's adversity with patience, trusting in God's good will, and keeping a good hope for the future life of eternal blessedness with God. Finally, they live thankfully, grateful for life's beauty and for the many signs in it of God's wise care.

A God Who Chooses: Predestination

In referring to Christian believers (the main audience Calvin addresses in most of his theological writings), I have been using, as a shorthand, pronouns in the first person plural ("we," "us"). If we count ourselves among the society of Christians, these pronouns may make the message of redemption sound fairly inclusive. But is it? Who comes under the heading of this "we"? How can we be so sure that *we* are included in the "we" who are on the way to eternal blessedness (as opposed to a far less pleasant destination)?

Faced with these kinds of questions, Calvin always wanted to offer assurance that we can be confident that we belong in the group headed in the right direction. God has rescued us from the wastebasket that our sin put us into. The teaching with which his name is so often associated, predestination, helps to assure us of this.

Or so he thought. In practice, the idea that God predestines, eternally ("before" all time), some to eternal salvation and all others to eternal damnation led more than a few of Calvin's readers and hearers to scratch their heads in wonder, awe, and fear. Others simply threw up their hands in disgust.

As we look at what Calvin believed about predestination, it is important to recognize that he didn't invent the doctrine. Orthodox theologians (including Augustine and Thomas Aquinas) had developed similar doctrines. But the church always tended to tone down the more explicit versions of predestinarian thinking, mainly because they didn't seem to do much for God's image. The predestinating God looked rather more like a thuggish concentration camp commandant toying with helpless lives than anything worthy of devotion and love. Why in the world then would Calvin insist on a picture of God whose work among creatures is based on an irrevocable "double decree"?

For Calvin, the answer to questions about the doctrine could be found (as usual) in Scripture. But one might look elsewhere, too, for some clues. We might look, for example, at the disparate experience of people's lives. Some people clearly make progress, of the spiritual and moral sort, in life. But others seem to be lost souls who simply can't get it right and show no sign of God's redemptive work in their lives. This evidence doesn't prove to us that the "successes" are God's chosen while the "failures" are not. Still, it speaks of the way in which God's grace seems to be unequally distributed.

What explains this "diversity"? The testimony offered in Scripture is that God has chosen some persons and rejected others. Is that a gloomy picture? No, Calvin thinks. It is not really different from the message of God's unfathomable mercy and grace that he has been concerned to stress from the beginning. What is the basis of my salvation? Is it a decision I make? The quality of my inner life? My moral worthiness? No. (And thank goodness for that: I am unable to make the right decision; my inner life is a cesspool; morally, I stink.) The basis of my salvation is not my free decision but God's. That divine decision is not a temporal choice based on a temporary whim; it is not subject to change. It is God's eternal determination—something that is absolutely reliable. That is why the Bible speaks of us as being chosen "in Christ before the foundation of the world" (Eph. 1:4) and of how "grace was given to us in Christ Jesus before the ages began" (2 Tim. 1:9). The message we find spoken through these passages, and in the broader narratives of the Old and New Testaments, of an electing God who chooses an elect people rings in the ears of people of faith as good news. Breaking the cycle of anxious self-scrutiny ("Am I good enough?") and arrogant self-congratulation ("Look how good I am!") with the recognition that salvation comes through "God's mere generosity," it elicits from its hearers a grateful response. Or at least it should.

Then why do so many scratch their heads when they hear this version of the message? Mainly, Calvin thinks, because they are not content to listen to the biblical witness and to hear it as good news for them. They (and perhaps we) want to go beyond what Scripture says and inquire into the "secret and hidden counsels of God." Who is elect? Who isn't? Is Uncle Frank? Aunt Minnie? Cousin Eustace? And what about me? It seems to some that if there is such a thing as an eternal divine decree, then it ought to be subject to the U.S. government's Freedom of Information Act. Curious (or inquiring) minds want to know! What exactly is in those documents?

In Calvin's view, God's will is, essentially, mysterious. That means that the workings of the mind of God are not accessible to us. What we do have access to is the "information" God has disclosed in the word and in Jesus Christ. That information is released on a need-to-know basis. We have in the Bible, in other words, reliable testimony to God's will *as it pertains to us*. But we have no other source beyond this, no text titled *Everything You Always Wanted to Know about God's Will . . . But Were Afraid to Ask*, and our limited understanding does not equip us to analyze God's will independent of an authoritative source. Calvin believes that when we ignore this, not respecting God's mystery, and try to "burst into the hidden chambers of the divine wisdom," we open ourselves up to enormous psychic and spiritual distress. We end up staring into an "abyss"—a vision of a universe devoid of meaning, a life without purpose or hope, a terrifying God of sheer power.

This inability to be satisfied with mystery and confine speculation to the limits of Scripture also accounts for the specific objections raised to this doctrine. For example, predestination makes God seem unfair and unjust. It cannot be right, can it, for God to decide the destiny of every person without reference to their moral worth? But, Calvin asks, what conception of justice can we use to judge the one who is the source of all justice? Of course we do have ordinary notions of fairness that we can and do use to judge cases of conflict or inequity. But in order to judge, one has to have access to all the information. Do we have sufficient information to assess the fairness of God's dealing with the whole of the human creation? Calvin thinks not. In any case, ordinary rules of justice, if applied to sinful human beings, would require severe punishment *for all*, obviating any extension of mercy to any portion of the fallen creation. This shows us that something is flawed in our procedure when we set about to assess the fairness of God's acts. We are not in a position to know why God acts in the ways God does; we certainly cannot claim, Calvin thinks, that any act of God could be wrong or unjust.

But what of these other, related, objections:

- Doesn't this picture of predestination remove responsibility from human beings? (We can't be held responsible for how we turn out if the way we develop is determined by God.)
- Wouldn't it lead to moral complacency? (No point in striving for moral improvement if my fate is already decided.)
- Won't it undermine any desire to preach and spread the gospel? (What good can preaching do if people are already chosen for one or another final destination?)

We are responsible, says Calvin, because our sin is a consequence of our choice and the fallen nature humanity itself chose. Of course, Calvin also wants to say that these choices were determined (and not simply allowed) by God. But God also ordains that the choices humans make will be genuinely theirs, and so their punishment will be just. We should consider ourselves responsible then for what we do, and complacency would be a very poor choice of attitude. It certainly is the case, says Calvin, that our destinies are established already in God's mind. But we don't have access to that particular database. We *do* know, however, based upon Scripture, that God's timeless election of human beings plays itself out in our time and place. People are called by God, through the preaching of God's word. Some respond to that word and some do not. If we receive God's call and experience God's kindness in forgiveness and regeneration, then we have strong grounds for thinking of ourselves as among God's chosen. If, on the other hand, we say, "Why bother responding to the gospel message if everything is already decided?"—well, that's pretty good evidence that we might be in the other club. (Go ahead. Choose your attitude.) So why preach? Preaching is the instrument God uses to work out, in time, God's election, drawing to God those who, from eternity, are bound for eternal blessedness. So preaching does make a difference, but not in the sense that it alters a divine plan. It makes a difference because it changes lives and participates in God's own work of bringing into being a community of faith, hope, and love.

Is this a harsh doctrine? In some ways, perhaps. Calvin was less concerned than many to soften the hard edges of this teaching, primarily because he was so intent on championing the message of God's unmerited grace. The kindness of God, and not anything we do, is the basis of our salvation. Too often, Calvin believed, the edges were softened in order to pay compliments to human nature or to suggest that there really might be something we can contribute to our reconciliation with God.

That kind of softening was not only theologically incorrect, thought Calvin, but also spiritually dangerous.

If it seems harsh to some ears, it is important to keep in mind that it was intended to be soothing. In fact (despite the objections of some), many of Calvin's contemporaries found it so. Calvin himself, we know, found enormous comfort in the message of God's election. Rather than having to stare into the abyss of a God of undomesticated power or, equally frightening, having to consider whether or not we are morally or spiritually fit for salvation, this teaching assured Christians that their salvation was certain, as it was willed by God "before the foundation of the world." It was comforting to those who had faith, since, as Calvin said, faith is the confirmation of election. Should they be troubled, still, by anxiety, they could and should look not to what they themselves possessed but to Christ. Christ, the "author of salvation," after all, is the one who reflects most clearly their election, showing them the face of the benevolent God, in whom is "no harshness . . . and no bitterness."[7]

In some interpretations of Calvin, predestination is understood to be the defining theme of his theology. It was not. For example, Calvin did not discuss the doctrine at all in the summary of his theological thinking that was intended to be most broadly available to laypersons in his time—his catechism. And he did not highlight it in his *Institutes*. He felt the teaching was valuable and important. But it needed to have the right context. He found that context in the final edition of the *Institutes*, placing it toward the end of the book dealing with "The Way in Which We Receive the Grace of Christ." Calvin meant to say that this is not a philosophical, speculative, or abstract idea; it is simply the teaching that confirms for us that God's free grace is the eternal foundation of our salvation, and—in the words of John Newton—"grace will lead me home."[8]

The Fourth Book: The Outward Means of Care

In Book 2 of the *Institutes*, Calvin deals with the objective facts of redemption. In Book 3, he turns to the subjective experience of the individual, grasped by God's grace. In the fourth and final book, he turns from that inner experience to look at the outer conditions that form the setting in which grace works. In the process, he also challenges any idea we might have that salvation and the Christian life are simply individual and private matters. The matrix of God's care in the world is communal. And so, as Calvin continues to tell the story of how God's grace works to restore human beings to wholeness and bring them into fellowship with God, he has to look at the communities that God fashions and through which God works to sustain them in life and prepare them for a life of blessedness. The first and most important of these is the church.

Mother of All the Godly

Calvin was a theologian of the church. That is, he was at home in the church. He thought the well-being of the church was worth the toil he devoted to it. Even though he broke with the ecclesiastical institution in which he was reared and witnessed a series of painful fractures among Christian communions, he continued to believe in the universal (catholic) church. Even though his struggle to find an authentic expression of that church in Geneva was fraught with enormous difficulties, he knew that the church was not dispensable. That conviction comes through loud and clear when Calvin discusses what the church is, how it functions, and how it is to be organized.

As in so many things, in his reflection on the church, Calvin stands in the tradition of Augustine. Augustine's main contribution to thinking about the church came in his dealings with those in his native North Africa who had joined the Donatist movement. The Donatists were Christians who had severed relations with the Catholic Church because they believed its clergy and the church as a whole were morally compromised. Donatism was a sectarian movement, an attempt to establish a church of the pure. Against the Donatists, Augustine argued that the church should really *be* catholic. "Catholic," in his view, was not simply a proper name but a descriptive term meaning universal, inclusive, embracing all. This broad, inclusive, worldwide church would, inevitably, include some who were not exactly pure. There would be some tares (or weeds) mixed in with the wheat (as in Jesus' parable in Matthew 13:24–30). But God would attend to the harvest, or the separating out of the good from the bad, in God's own time. The business of the church was to be the united body of all those who professed Christ and to be the arena in which the wheat, at least, would experience God's grace.

But, we might ask, can it really be the church if we have too high a proportion of tares to wheat? Don't the Donatists have a point: Shouldn't the church *really* be a collection of faithful people and not admit just anyone who feels like coming through the doors in order to look for good business connections, a better public image, or just a comfortable pew to doze in? Yes, Calvin says, the church should be, and in a sense is, the community of all truly faithful people. The church understood in this more exclusive sense is what he calls the *invisible church*. That church is known only to God. We can't measure the boundaries of this church. For one thing, it includes all the redeemed—past, present, future—and we can't see all those people. But we know that such a church exists, says Calvin, and Christians can be confident that God will ultimately make this church apparent.

Although he thinks it's important, Calvin doesn't think there is much more to be said about the invisible church. We can say a good deal more about the *visible church*, which is the institution of our daily experience. It includes, of course, all those weeds as well as the wheat, but it is this expression of the church—an imperfect gathering of faithful and not-so-faithful people—that is the object of the Holy Spirit's care and nourishing in our history. It is the place where we experience God's grace and learn about God and ourselves. Calvin borrows from Cyprian of Carthage (c. 200–258) one of his favorite images for the church, the idea that the church is like a mother: "There is no other way to enter into life unless this mother conceive us in her womb, nourish us at her breast, and lastly, unless she keep us under her care and guidance." Equally important, from his point of view, this nurturing church is a constant presence in human history. It did not come to life only with the advent of Jesus or following his resurrection; the church, like the Word, is as old as God's history with God's people. Thus, ancient Israel does not stand outside the church, nor is it a vague prefiguring of the church; Israel is the church.

Discerning the Church

One of the main challenges Calvin and his contemporaries faced when thinking about the visible church centered around the question, Where is it now? The schism between Catholics and Protestants, the splintering within Protestant churches, and the mutual denunciations that came from virtually all sides meant that it wasn't terribly easy to tell which collection of Christians really represented the church. Was there some way to distinguish the genuine item from a cheap imitation?

Indeed there was, said Calvin. A collection of Christians embodies the church if among them (1) God's word is truly preached and reverently heard and (2) the sacraments are administered according to Christ's institution. Defining the church this way signaled a decisive departure from the Catholic insistence that the church was constituted only by apostolic succession (the great continuity of ordination from Jesus to Peter and the disciples, to subsequent bishops and priests on down to the present). It also was intended to supply a fairly inclusive definition. Along the lines of Augustine, Calvin didn't think one would ever be justified in walking away from the church, thus defined. And when one did walk away from an institution that called itself the church, he had better have some pretty good reasons for doing so.

That warning would seem to apply to Calvin himself, wouldn't it? As a young man, hadn't he left the Catholic Church? Wasn't he a bit of a Donatist himself? Maybe. But Calvin didn't see it that way. He left an institution that he believed had ceased to preach the gospel and whose sacraments were distortions of God's word. In his view, he had not left the church at all but simply been led by God to the place where God's church was presently embodied. He came to believe, in other words, that the Catholic Church was no longer the true church, although he did insist that pockets of the true church could, and did, survive within Catholicism.

In settling on the two signs or marks of the church (the Word preached and heard and the sacraments rightly administered), Calvin was clearly departing from a Catholic vision. But, as Calvin warned about leaving the fellowship of the true visible church, he also resisted the position of other Christians of his time, those who had broken with the church of Rome and then found the need also to distance themselves from churches associated with reformers such as Luther and Calvin. The most significant of these groups, the Anabaptists, were, in some sense, the Donatists of their day. They rejected infant baptism and advocated the separation of the church from the influences of a corrupt social and political culture. Because they viewed the church as a gathered community of the holy, called to be pure, "without a spot or wrinkle" (Eph. 5:27), they practiced rigorous discipline to censure their members for their failings and to remove incorrigible sinners from the church. Calvin rejected this rigorist view of the church, but it is possible he learned a thing or two from the Anabaptists.

Order in the Church

If Calvin had learned from the Anabaptists, we would find their influence in his arguments for a disciplined church. In his view, although Augustine was right—the church includes both tares and wheat—the true church also has means available, devised by God and taught by Jesus himself, for dealing with the tares when they become too unruly or with the wheat when they forget their manners and start behaving like tares. A study of the New Testament shows that procedures of discipline were developed in the early church to deal with conflicts between church members. In Calvin's view, these procedures involved a council of elders representing the church, a deliberative body that exercised a kind of ecclesiastical judicial authority. They would hear cases in which disputants could not overcome a personal disagreement, as well as look into instances of scandalous behavior. Such a council's power was limited. It could not coerce offenders, but it might persuade with various tools, from gentle admonition to exclusion from the Lord's Supper (the most serious punishment).

The council of elders took shape in Geneva as the consistory, the morals court made up of the church's elders and the pastors. Calvin made clear that this body was not to get carried away in its zeal to establish moral purity. Its job was not to separate the tares from the wheat. That was God's job, and only God was equipped to perform it. But the consistory certainly could work to keep order in the church. This demand for order was not simply an expression of Calvinist anal retentiveness. Like Paul's counsel to do everything in the church "decently and in order" (1 Cor. 14:40), Calvin's concern is born out of a conviction that only an ordered environment, in which reasoned deliberation can take place, is conducive to cultivating piety and expressing love. That is the basic aim of discipline, in Calvin's view: to hold together and strengthen the church as the body of Christ, a community that witnesses to and lives out Christ's love. So, for Calvin, discipline is not, as with the Donatists and Anabaptists, a means of creating a church of the pure. Calvin's church is a church of sinners, but it is a place where sin is being overcome through the preaching of the gospel. In his view, then, the ancient creeds that call the church "holy" are not incorrect. But instead of thinking of this holiness as an already accomplished fact, we ought to recognize it as the goal that God ultimately will achieve.

Discipline was important enough to Calvin that it almost became a third mark, or sign, of the church. Yet in the end, Calvin resisted elevating discipline to the level of preaching and the sacraments. In his view, the Word that is preached and exhibited sacramentally is the life force of the church, and so it is this word that establishes the church's identity. In Book 1, Calvin rejects the claim that the church's authority stands above the authority of God's word. That denial doesn't translate for him into a church without any authority. It does mean that the authority the church claims is entirely dependent on the Word.

This is one of the reasons Calvin tried to remain as close as possible to the text of Scripture when he identified offices in the church and devised a church structure. Although the interpretation of New Testament passages referring to official positions in the church was at the time, and remains, controvertible, Calvin thought that the early church recognized four principal, continuing offices: pastor, doctor, elder, and deacon. These were the offices he helped to institute in his order for the Genevan church, devised on his return to the city in 1541. The functions of church offices differ, in his view, but they all relate, in their various ways, to the word of God. Pastors are specifically charged with preaching the Word and tending to the care of souls. All others—doctors (in their teaching), elders (in tending to the moral and spiritual health of their brothers and sisters), and deacons (in serving the poor and disabled)—work to bring the substance of what God communicates in Scripture to bear on the common life of faithful Christians.

Signs, Sealed, Delivered

We have seen that Calvinism made a sharp break with the piety of Catholicism, with its strongly sacramental emphasis. That is, the view that God's actual presence could be found in the material of life—in the bodies of saints, in holy images or relics—was rejected by the Calvinists as unbiblical and an incitement to idolatry. We won't be surprised then to find that Calvin's way of treating the sacraments of the church is rather different from Catholic treatments. But if we expect to find Calvin rejecting the idea of sacraments altogether, then perhaps we will be surprised. In fact, he regarded the sacraments very highly. Like his fellow Protestants, he reduced the number of sacraments (the medieval church recognized seven) to two: baptism and the eucharist, or the Lord's Supper. That reduction was intended to recognize the symbolic acts that Jesus himself established or commanded his followers to continue to observe. It was not intended to reduce the church's emphasis on sacramental acts; instead, Calvin believed, it should focus attention on the practices of faith God intends for us.

Calvin's sacramental thought is worth attending to if only because it was at the center of a theological whirlwind in the sixteenth century. Reformers of various persuasions came virtually to blows over questions raised by these central Christian rites, and their differences posed insurmountable obstacles to peace among Christians in this period. Calvin's understanding of the sacraments played a pivotal role in these controversies, and his formulations left a profound impact on later thought and practice.

Calvin maintains that sacraments are important auxiliaries to the Word. They are important, first, because God has given them to humanity and commanded (in Scripture) their continued use. They are important, second, because when we look at the character of sacraments we can see what great value they have. They are visual reminders of the central messages God is concerned to communicate to creatures. And, like the written and preached Word, they are the media through which God communicates God's self to us. Calvin calls them instruments that "seal" on our consciences the promises spoken to us in God's word. So closely related are God's word and the sacraments entrusted to the church that Calvin believes Augustine was quite right to call a sacrament a kind of "visible word."

Augustine's other way of characterizing sacraments, "a sign of a sacred thing," furnished important language for the sixteenth-century Protestants who reflected on and argued about what sacraments are and how they work. The Swiss reformer Zwingli, in particular, emphasized that sacraments were no more than signs and should not be confused with the things they signify. That is, for example, the bread and wine used in the Lord's Supper are reminders of Jesus' body and blood and they call to mind his sacrificial death. But we shouldn't equate the bread with Jesus' actual body. Martin Luther, on the other hand, thought that the signs and the things they signify were joined together whenever a sacramental promise indicated such a joining. And so Jesus' declaration, "This is my body," stands as a promise that his very body is given to us in the bread of Communion.

Calvin's reflection on the sacraments as signs places him in between Zwingli and Luther. With Zwingli, Calvin maintains that the sign should not be confused with what it signifies. But the sign is not a simple reminder; with Luther, Calvin thinks that a sign conveys the reality to which it points. But against Luther, he thinks it's a mistake to identify the sign and the thing signified. Rather than thinking of the sign and the thing it signifies as separate (Zwingli, according to Calvin) or thinking of the thing signified being present *in* the sign and failing to distinguish sign from signified (Luther, according to Calvin), we should imagine God powerfully relating the two, making the signified thing available *through* (not in) the sign.

These ideas of signs and signified things anticipated a good deal of later, modern reflection on symbol theory and theories of language that came to be called semiotics, or the study of signs. In the way I have presented this, it may seem a bit abstract. Oddly enough, however, when these ideas were related directly to questions about baptism and the eucharist, laypersons of the sixteenth century, people without any formal theological training, actually paid attention! They cared, many of them passionately, about these matters, some of them giving their lives in defense of the particular convictions they held.

On the matter of baptism, Anabaptists—who were a small minority—suffered for their views more than just about anyone else. Although Calvin did not actively persecute Anabaptists, he did argue with them about the validity of infant baptism. As Zwingli had before him, Calvin maintained that the baptism of infants was justified because from ancient times it had been used as the rite through which children entered the church; it was the specifically Christian successor to the Jewish sacrament of circumcision. Calvin's defense of infant baptism fits well with his understanding of the church as the mother at whose breasts Christians are nourished. The church, conceived of this way, of course accepts the very young into its inner circle! The church doesn't wait for expressions of faith to appear, because baptism is the sign that marks God's claim on the infant and signifies the believing community's duty to nurture the child in and toward faith. Baptizing all infants whose parents are members of the community of faith also signals an inclusive understanding of the church in relation to its cultural environment. Unlike the Anabaptists, the church Calvin envisioned would reflect, embrace, and transform its society rather than being set apart from it.

Discussion of the Lord's Supper proved the most divisive of any theological matter, although Calvin did his best to state his understanding in a way that was both true to his reading of the Bible and potentially agreeable to as many of his contemporaries as possible. The theory of sign and signified thing was the crux of his interpretation. In the eucharist, the body and blood not only points to but actually delivers, communicates, or exhibits Jesus Christ to those who come to the Supper with faith. The bread and wine do not become Jesus Christ, but through these signs, and by means of the participants' faith, the Holy Spirit joins together in Communion believers on earth with the heavenly body of their Redeemer. How does this happen? It is a mystery too high for the human mind (even Calvin's) to grasp. But God promises it, and we should believe it. Calvin's interpretation, then, was an attempt to emphasize the real, spiritual union of Christians with Christ (this was something Luther was concerned about also) without requiring, as he says, that Christ "descend into bread."

This interpretation did not satisfy all those Calvin might have hoped to win over. However, he did manage to convince some Zwinglians to adopt a modified version of his approach. Lutherans were more reluctant to come on board. Catholics, who held firmly to the view of a real, bodily, sacramental presence (with only a few exceptions), rejected it entirely. Still, it supplied a way of talking about sacraments in general and the eucharist in particular that influenced profoundly a large number of Christians in Calvin's wake. Its influence reemerged in productive ways when Christians long separated over theological matters began talking again, in the mid-twentieth century, about ways to heal their divisions.

Balancing Power

The very last topic Calvin takes up in his *Institutes* concerns the nature of civil government, the duties of rulers, and the responsibilities of Christians toward political authority. It has to do, in other words, with politics and political power. We might be tempted to ask, Why is a theologian meddling in politics? Isn't this a bit outside his sphere of competence? Calvin might answer by noting that Scripture, the principal sourcebook for theological reflection, has a good deal to say about politics and the use of power. From ancient Israelite lawgiving, to the historical chronicles of the national experience of ancient Israel, to the prophets' witness to God's requirement for justice and compassion for the poor and oppressed, to the struggles of the early Christian communities to define the relation between their duty to God and to the emperor, both Old and New Testaments reflect a perennial concern to come to grips with the relationship between the demands of faith and the structures of power that organize daily life. Calvin lived in a time that could not really imagine the bifurcation of religion and public life that has become characteristic of modern experience. So it was entirely natural for him to examine political life in his account of Christian faith.

Calvin begins with an axiom that he believes is derived from Scripture: Civil government, like the church, is a gift of God and an expression of God's wise rule of the world. He reflects, in other words, the confident and hopeful stance toward political power suggested in Paul's advice to the Christians in Rome: "Let every person be subject to the governing authorities; for there is no authority except from God, and those authorities that exist have been instituted by God" (Rom. 13:1). Unlike later political philosophers who would view government as a necessary evil, Calvin viewed it as entirely beneficial: "It is God's servant for your good" (Rom. 13:4).

Were we to hear these judgments without any qualification, both Paul and Calvin would seem extremely naive. Didn't they have any experience of government? Of course they did. And both recognized that certain governments could do harm and that the relationship of persons of faith to political power could be a troubled one. Calvin had fled a repressive government in France and subsequently lived under a government with which he was frequently at odds. His main audience were members of an underground church living virtually, many of them, under a sentence of death on account of their faith. So the confidence expressed in the judgment that government is an instrument of God's care is not meant to be a rosy assessment. Instead, it reflects trust in God's providence.

In claiming this confidence, Calvin means to distance himself from those he calls "despisers of authority." These are the persons in the sixteenth century (Calvin thinks primarily of Anabaptist radicals) who believe that government can be done without, or that it must be overturned, or that—because government uses unchristian means of achieving its ends (such as coercion and violence)—Christians should avoid any association with it. Those who reject the state are guilty, he thinks, of ingratitude; they turn their backs on the good gift of public rule God has made available for our care. But Calvin is concerned also to distance himself from those who make the opposite error. These are persons who not only defend political power but try to increase its concentration in the hands of rulers and to extend governmental power into areas into which it has no business going. The "flatterers of princes," as Calvin calls them (he has in mind royal counselors or propagandists for the state), by convincing rulers that their power is unbounded, are guilty of idolatry. That is, they confuse limited human authority with the unlimited power of God. Christians need to find a middle way between these two extremes: a way that recognizes government as a power intended to serve human needs and produce what is good, while guarding against an untenable expansion of governmental power.

But what of the perennially vexing question of church and state? Since Calvin claims the state is an instrument of God's care, as is the church, how is he going to manage the relationship between the two? First, in order to address that question, we need to recognize that most people in the sixteenth century assumed a much closer relation between church and state than most of us today probably do. The models mapping this relation generally proposed a hierarchy: Either the church was above the state (the argument, understandably, of some of the more ambitious popes and their supporters) or the state was above the church. The Swiss Protestant cities closest to Geneva put into practice a version of that latter ranking. Magistrates were to have oversight of all matters, including religion and the life of the church.

By contrast, Calvin's model rejected a simple hierarchy in favor of complementarity: Church and state are distinct entities that serve distinct but complementary aims. The church tends to the spiritual or inner condition of the person; the state handles political or outward things. Each power needs the other. The state needs the church because without the feeding of the soul that the church attends to, there is no basis for public peace. The church needs the state because without the peace, order, and justice civil government imposes, religion cannot thrive. Proposing a symbiotic relation translated, in Calvin's practice, to resisting the claims of rulers to interfere in church affairs. That practice, as we've seen, brought him into conflict with some of Geneva's magistrates. The main source of the tension, however, was the discrepancy between the (Zwinglian) practice of the Swiss cities (most notably Bern, Geneva's military protector, whose rulers wanted Geneva to conform to its way of doing things) and the view Calvin propounded. Calvin's success in introducing an alternative model in Geneva helped to pave the way for later developments, in which the church's business would be increasingly disengaged from the business of government.

The separation of church and state that Thomas Jefferson (1743–1826) later proposed for the new American nation was not quite what Calvin had in mind, however. In an age that could not have contemplated the value of secularism, when religious symbols were the basis of social and cultural unity and when it was largely assumed that no society that tolerated a wide array of religious practice and belief could survive, Calvin (with the majority of his contemporaries) assumed

1. that societies would be more or less religiously homogeneous, and
2. that governments could appropriately establish and defend the church, protect "the outward worship of God," and in so doing establish a form of civil righteousness.

Government could and should make society (outwardly) good (or some approximation of that), just as the church aimed at caring for people's souls so that they could be (inwardly) good (or on the way to goodness). Needless to say, the way this vision was implemented in the sixteenth century shows that the values of religious toleration and cultural pluralism were not yet appreciated in Calvin's world.

What then is my duty as a Christian toward government? Calvin says that I should be thankful for it, recognizing that it is as necessary to my life as "bread, water, sun, and air." And, respecting the existing political structure, I should make use of and participate in the structures it puts in place (I pay taxes, I make use of the courts—but judiciously), and I should be obedient to its rule. What responsibility does the ruler have? He or she is responsible to God, who is the source of all authority. God will punish unjust rulers, but private citizens cannot take that task on themselves (Rom. 13:2). Under certain constitutions, tyrants can be resisted and overthrown using the proper constitutional means. But in no instance can a Christian go outside the law to resist duly constituted political authority.

That emphasis on obedience *seems* to leave governmental power free to do pretty much as it pleases. But Calvin's earliest readers didn't see it that way. There were more than a few revolutionaries among the Calvinists. They believed that when kings forget their limits and command things contrary to what God requires, then resistance was not only appropriate but necessary. As Calvin himself said, "We ought rather to spit in their faces than obey them when they are so shameless as to want to despoil God of his right and as it were occupy his throne, as if they could drag him out of heaven." When conflict of this kind arose, as the apostle Peter had said, "We must obey God rather than human beings" (Acts 5:29).[9]

In the prefatory letter to Francis I that headed up every edition of the *Institutes*, Calvin meant to assure the king and other representatives of civil authority not only that the evangelical Christians he represented were theologically orthodox but that they posed no political threat. He was not entirely successful in conveying that message. In the final book of his work, he does underline the fact that Reformed Christians take seriously and deeply value the outward institutions (church and state) through which God governs life. But he also, implicitly and explicitly, furnished ways of criticizing these very institutions. This was appropriate, from Calvin's point of view. Human fallenness meant that institutions would fall into error and cause harm. Sanctifying error and criminal violence did no one any good. So some way of measuring church and state against God's vision for both had to be achieved. Characteristically, Calvin believed an interpretation of the Bible supplied the right means for doing this.

In Sum . . .

And now we come to the end of the tale Calvin was concerned to tell. Here is one way of summing it up: The Christian faith derives from God, who speaks to us, invites us and draws us into the society of Christ, turns us away from sin and toward holiness, and rules our world, guiding and supporting us through earthly instruments of care. The Christian can trust God and should rely on God for all things. Her confidence should not be in herself, in the world, or in her earthly condition. She should be thankful for all good gifts, especially the gift of God's kindness, but she should not rely on other goods easily taken away. Though she may be vulnerable to the exigencies of an apparently muddled history, she knows that a wise God rules all things. And so she is a confident actor in a world whose source and destination is the good its Creator intends.

That broad summary would have been acceptable to many Christians of Calvin's time. Difficulties came, however, because of the dramatic details necessary to flesh out the synopsis. Let's turn now to look at some of the more significant controversies that Calvin's details provoked.

Chapter Four

Trials and Travail

Calvin's Fire

God may be in the details, as the modernist architect Mies van der Rohe said. But to judge from popular characterizations, the devil must have devised the theological details of the *Institutes of the Christian Religion*. "Sheer diabolism," one late nineteenth-century commentator called them. And if this describes his thought, can Calvin as its author have been anything less than diabolical? References abound in popular literature to Calvin as intolerant, a heartless and sadistic tyrant, "more despotic" than the medieval popes, a man whose "sternness was that of the judge who dooms a criminal to the gallows."[10]

This sort of depiction has become standard fare, but its roots can be found in the complaints of Calvin's earliest critics. Theodore Beza (1516–1605), Calvin's successor and his first biographer, referred to these when he noted that many had charged him with being "far too choleric," which meant, generally, hot-tempered. The charge also suggested, according to the classical medical theory assumed by Calvin and others of his time, that he had an imbalance in the four basic humors (bodily fluids governing health and disposition). Hence a choleric temperament: angry, intolerant, dictatorial. Beza did not deny this charge, even though his own characterizations (and Calvin's self-descriptions) suggested he was somewhat more melancholic (thin, pale, sensitive, introverted) than classically choleric. Instead, Beza argued that Calvin's "vehemence"—his quick intelligence, incisive wit, passionate pursuit of the truth, and confidence in the rightness of his own convictions—had served the cause of the gospel extraordinarily well. If there was fire in Calvin (and Beza admitted that with age and illness he became increasingly prickly), it had served a prophetic purpose. God had used him as a mouthpiece, not only to enable faithful Christians to see the light but to force "the obstinate and perverse to bend under the great power of God."[11]

Beza, in other words, found Calvin's temperament perfectly suited to the controversies of the time. It was Calvin's involvement in controversies that provided the initial evidence for accusations of despotism and a temper out of control. Calvin's passion came through in many confrontations with an assortment of adversaries. His political opponents in Geneva were principal adversaries, but there were many others as well. He wrote against a variety of groups, known by the derogatory labels he or others gave them—Papists, Anabaptists, Spiritual Libertines, Nicodemites.[12] He spent years in unproductive debate with Lutheran critics of his theology of the Lord's Supper. In all these controversies, Calvin's "vehemence" is apparent. But in none was his reputation damaged as severely as it was by his involvement in two high-profile criminal cases: the trials in Geneva of two persons on charges of heresy, Jerome Bolsec and Michael Servetus. Because this involvement became the main source for the enduring images of Calvin's intolerance, vindictiveness, and brutality, these trials are worth a closer look.

Arguing Predestination

It seems that when Jerome Bolsec first came to significant public attention in Geneva, he had been stewing for some time over the way Calvin referred to God's predestination. He let his views be known at the regular Friday meeting of Geneva's Congregation (the weekly Bible study session and theological seminar) on October 16, 1551.

Bolsec was a physician and a former monk. Although no longer a man of the cloth, he had deep theological interests; and although in other respects he counted himself a respectable Protestant, on this business of predestination he thought Calvin and the other Genevan pastors were plain wrong. For one thing, he said, if they teach that God determines before a person acts that that person will be sinful, will not benefit from grace, and will be damned, then that makes God look pretty bad. God is capricious and God is the author of sin—a silly idea.

He expressed these views freely at the Congregation, Calvin being away from the meeting. But Calvin slipped in halfway through Bolsec's discourse, and when Bolsec finished, Calvin stood up and gave an elaborate, lengthy, and (in the view of his supporters) a devastatingly effective rebuttal. Because Bolsec not only attacked Calvin but claimed that the preaching of the Genevan church was in serious error, he was immediately arrested. The charge filed fell under the category of heresy, and so, according to Geneva's criminal code, the case went before the city magistrates.

It was not an easy case for a group of men with little experience in technical theological matters to hear. Calvin testified in defense of his own position: He denied the most serious of Bolsec's charges, that he made God the author of sin. Hadn't Bolsec read what Calvin had written? Calvin had straightforwardly denied that God was the author of sin! Still, the implication seemed to be there: How could you get away from attributing *some* sort of responsibility to God for the wickedness humans do if everything is ultimately ordained by God? Calvin worried that the argument was taking a scholastic turn rather than keeping to the bounds Scripture prescribes; Bolsec, after all, was a monkish, former Parisian scholastic! He was trying to make God's election depend on what humans do—they have the freedom to accept or reject the gospel—so as to protect the idea of human responsibility. But, according to Calvin, this view overturned everything Augustine had achieved in his debate with Pelagius. It made human beings responsible for their own salvation.

Puzzled over the deep questions with which they had to deal, the magistrates called for a consultation with their allies in the Swiss Protestant cities. The responses came back, and their verdict was inconclusive. Bolsec was supported by no one. A few were enthusiastically supportive of Calvin. But the Zwinglian cities poked a few jabs at Calvin; they were not terribly pleased with his predestinarian view either. Not entirely confident that the case was theologically crystal clear, the Genevan court decided to side with their pastor Calvin, who had made his case passionately, and against Bolsec, who had also expressed himself with passion but had (in the process) slandered Geneva, its ministers, and its doctrine. For holding an erroneous theological position and refusing to recant and retract his charge against Geneva's ministers, he was sentenced to "perpetual exile" from the city.

Banished from Geneva, Bolsec went to Bern and from there continued to attack Calvin until the city's magistrates finally asked him to leave in 1555. In the same year, they prohibited further discussion of predestination. Bolsec eventually returned to the Catholic fold and did his part to try to check the spread of Calvinism by writing, after Calvin had died, a scathing and highly inventive exposé of the life and personal proclivities of his erstwhile enemy.

Calvin's response to Bolsec's first charges, Bolsec's trial, and the Small Council's verdict was to give even more attention than before to the doctrine that was the source of the controversy. Calvin was disappointed that Geneva's magistrates had not given him more enthusiastic support, and he felt under attack from the Zwinglian Swiss. Typically, when facing a challenge to a position he had taken, Calvin's impulse was to strengthen his arguments and amplify his evidence. Yet, even as he was concerned to defend the view of predestination he was convinced Scripture demanded, he never pushed the doctrine to a place of prominence in his theological scheme. That move was left to his successors. Still, he gave it more prominence than many were comfortable with.

Servetus and a Three-Headed Dog

On August 13, 1553, Michael Servetus was arrested in Geneva on a charge of heresy. According to the allegations, he had denied the doctrine of the Trinity and the practice of infant baptism.

Servetus was a new arrival in the city. He was on the run, fleeing a conviction on similar charges of heresy in the French city of Vienne. Like Bolsec, he was a physician, but also a bit of a Renaissance man. He was extraordinarily well-read, especially in sources that could get a good Christian into trouble in the sixteenth century. He had sampled early Christian heterodox (Gnostic) texts and Jewish rabbinical writings and was familiar with traditions of mystical and esoteric philosophy. A pioneer in medical research, he is credited with having discovered the pulmonary circulation of the blood. But his real passion seems to have been theological. He wrote and published three works, anonymously, whose arguments put him (possibly) well ahead of his time in terms of their critical stance toward the history of Christian doctrines and (definitely) far out of the mainstream of tolerated theological positions. Prior to emerging in Geneva, Servetus had lived much of his life under assumed names. He knew he would be in big trouble should anyone connect him with the views he held and the books he wrote. Still, he ended up in 1553 in a city that employed the man who could do just that.

The charges lodged against Servetus were more serious, in the context of sixteenth-century understandings, than any other accusation of heresy previously heard in Geneva. Bolsec had disputed Calvin's version of a doctrine many of his fellow Christians were already uncomfortable with. Servetus, on the other hand, was denying outright a doctrine long held to be essential to Christian faith. (To him, the Trinity was an outrageous perversion, an absurd monstrosity like Cerberus, the three-headed dog of classical mythology.) More serious still, he had written and published his views—evidence that he not only held erroneous views but intended to propagate them. Servetus probably would have been executed by any number of European jurisdictions in his time. But for one reason or another he came to Geneva. When the Genevan magistrates gave him the option of returning to Catholic Vienne, where he had already been condemned (and burned in effigy), to take his chances there, Servetus chose to stay in Geneva and await its judicial decision.

When the news came it was, of course, not good news for him. The magistrates, recognizing that they had a high-profile, and possibly very sensitive, case on their hands, consulted once again with their Swiss Protestant allies. The responses Geneva received all supported conviction and capital punishment. The magistrates, in any case, probably felt under pressure to make an example of Servetus. They were already nervous because their city had been portrayed as a haven for all of Europe's most dangerous heretics. In fact, by the standards of the time, Geneva had been lenient with those convicted of heresy, banishing them rather than putting them to death. So Servetus was sentenced to death by burning. Calvin tried to persuade the magistrates to impose a more humane punishment—beheading—but the council was unwilling to deviate from the traditional method of executing heretics. Servetus, attended by the visiting Farel, who served him as pastoral counselor, was burned alive, together with his books. He went to his death, convinced of the truth of his beliefs (stubbornly firm in his tragic error, according to Farel) and exclaiming at the last, "O Jesus, Son of the Eternal God, have pity on me!" The theological error was evident in the word placement: "Eternal Son of God" would have signified that Jesus was fully divine and qualified Servetus as an orthodox Trinitarian.

Calvin seldom appears a sympathetic figure in the telling of this story. But some versions make him look worse than others, for no reason (apparently) than the animus of the teller. Calvin was not, as some would have it, Servetus's prosecutor, judge, and executioner. He did play a very important role in the affair. Calvin had had a long acquaintance, through correspondence, with Servetus. He had tried in his letters to persuade his correspondent to reconsider his views but without success. He was Servetus's main accuser and the chief expert witness against him. However, it probably did not require a theologian of Calvin's caliber to lead the court to its guilty verdict. Servetus's views were plain enough and sufficiently out of the mainstream of normative doctrine to convict him in almost any sixteenth-century court. Calvin was not a judge in the case—it was, after all (as with Bolsec), a criminal and secular case in which Calvin, limited to his role in the church, had no authority and could not serve as arbiter. For the same reason, Calvin could not have executed Servetus. The magistrates who heard the case—most of them, at the moment, unhappy with Calvin and his policies—were in no mood to cede any judicial or executive power to this French pastor.

If Calvin does not look good in the record of the case, it probably has something to do with the vehemence of his testimony against a heretic. Calvin seems initially to have been sympathetic toward Servetus. But when he appeared to be beyond persuading, Calvin's antipathy was all too apparent. The vehemence might also have been a result of Calvin's sense that he himself might well have been vulnerable to charges of heresy in the course of the trial. This is not quite as far-fetched as it sounds. Servetus had for some time been propounding views that contradicted Calvin's teachings. He had written to Calvin, trying to persuade him that he was wrong. At a time (1553) when Calvin was going head to head with Geneva's rulers over the relation of church and state, when the majority of the magistrates were his political opponents, Servetus appears on the scene. When he is accused of heresy, he turns the table on his accuser and claims Calvin is the heretic! As it turned out, Calvin was fairly secure. But in the midst of the trial, he could not be quite so confident of the outcome.

An additional reason for Calvin's not coming off terribly well in this affair has less to do with him and more to do with us. That is, we likely hold Calvin to standards set by values common to our time. Calvin was not as tolerant of divergent views as he should have been. But in this respect, he represents an age that knew little of tolerance. However we assess Calvin's actions, we should bear in mind that Servetus's execution was not exceptional for the time. Sixteenth-century Europe (and Europe prior to that time) was harshly intolerant of religious deviance—especially when the deviation was thought to be serious enough to threaten the peace and purity of the church. The medieval church had made a standard practice of handing over to the state unrepentant heretics to receive capital punishment. Perhaps the single feature of the case that distinguishes the proceedings from many other similar actions of the period is the attention the Genevan magistrates gave to due process. They weighed the evidence for some time and were careful to solicit opinions from outside Geneva. Standard treatment for heretics in the hottest periods of repression in Catholic France or Spain in the 1550s involved summary justice, practically in front of the stake. And in contrast to a number of other territories where such things were common, in Calvin's lifetime Geneva executed only one person for heterodox views.

Considering all these things probably will not cause us to see a kinder and gentler Calvin in the man who served as Servetus's main accuser. But it might help us to see him as a man of his time.

Calvin probably had not intended to use the ashes of an adversary for personal advancement. Still, the trial, execution, and aftermath does seem to have benefited Calvin. To many observers, he emerged from the Servetus affair in a better position, both in Geneva and abroad. Not only had he successfully defended himself and his teaching; he looked to be an extremely able defender of classical Christian doctrine. And so the unfortunate Servetus helped to prepare the way not only for Calvin's eventual victory over his Genevan opponents but for his emergence after this victory as a powerful force in an international movement of Christian reform.

Calvinism Rising

Theological victories over opponents such as Bolsec and Servetus and the political victory in Geneva left Calvin free to attend to matters elsewhere and transformed this border city on the edge of the Alps into what one observer called a Protestant Rome. It became, that is, the center of a vital movement and ministry on behalf of a new vision of the church—a vision that coincided with Calvin's.

Several developments contributed to this transformation. First, Calvin, who had been lecturing to and training students for many years, was finally able to establish formally the educational institution of his dreams. The Genevan Academy, founded in 1558, was set up to offer advanced education, particularly for the training of pastors. With an immediate and large influx of students (many from France) wishing to be trained in the humanistic and evangelically oriented curriculum set up by Calvin and the institution's new rector, Theodore Beza, the Academy quickly became one of the most important places for the shaping of the Reformed movement. Calvin's theology and his emphasis on rigorous training in the linguistic skills necessary to interpret the Bible in Hebrew and Greek became the centerpiece of the education these pastors-in-training received. Through them, the mark of Calvin's values and his ways of thinking were imprinted deeply on the life of churches throughout Europe.

The establishment of education in Geneva served the second significant development in Calvin's latter years—the beginning of a hugely successful missionary undertaking. Although Calvin had European-wide and worldwide interests, France was the field upon which most attention was concentrated. No Reformed church had been established in France before 1555. However, Reformed movements of various types had had some success there, and thanks both to Calvin's prolific writing and the publishing industry that had become a major Genevan industry since Calvin's arrival, the evangelical-minded in France had been well supplied with Bibles and religious tracts. Calvin's extensive correspondence also helped to cultivate communities of faith throughout France that looked to Calvin and to Geneva for guidance. Still, these nascent Reformed communities lacked the rudiments of an ecclesiastical structure—until 1555. Within the next several years, Geneva sent out scores of able and well-trained pastors to preach and organize churches that operated according to the form of discipline Calvin had introduced. By 1559, a national church structure was implemented to organize as a body the congregations that were spreading throughout the country. (There were more than a thousand, and perhaps as many two thousand, by 1562). A Presbyterian, Reformed Church of France was born.

Calvin's influence in these years was not limited to France, however. His theology and his view of church order were gaining a significant number of adherents in various parts of Europe. In Scotland, England, the Netherlands, and the German Palatinate, the impact of Calvin's thinking was powerfully apparent in the realms of church and politics. But it must have given Calvin special satisfaction to observe the inroads being made in his native land in the last years of his life. In fact, by 1561, Calvin and his colleagues entertained cautious hopes that the royal family might be coming around to adopting (or maybe simply tolerating) what was now being called the "Reformed religion." French Calvinists, who came to be called Huguenots, were becoming an important faction in France. The queen mother, Catherine de Medici, recognized this and made some overtures to them. But hopes for a peaceful solution to religious differences were dashed when ecumenical efforts failed and, after a massacre of Protestant worshipers by Catholic troops in March 1562, the country erupted in civil war—the first of the so-called Wars of Religion that would extend over the next four decades.

Calvin Declining

As his movement was waxing, however, Calvin was waning. He had suffered for some time from numerous illnesses, and just as his many years of labor were beginning to bear fruit, his body was giving way. He suffered from gout, kidney stones, tuberculosis, and intestinal parasites, among other ailments. Yet he continued at his work, even when in considerable pain. In his last years he would be carried into the pulpit or the lecture hall, but in February 1564 he gave his last lecture and last sermon. Keeping at what little work he could do from his bed, he continued to decline, to the point at which it seemed appropriate to begin to say his goodbyes.

He saw Geneva's magistrates on April 27, encouraged them to be steadfast in the service of the reformation and begged their forgiveness for his weaknesses and his "far too vehement natural disposition." And yet, as he said, he would not stoop to hypocrisy and deny that God had worked some good through him. His fellow pastors were summoned the next day to hear his admonition to avoid unnecessary changes and to build on the gains made through their labor together. His good friend Farel (they had become extremely close since Farel's frightening imprecation that kept him, reluctantly, in Geneva) was told in a letter a few days later that, as every breath was now coming with difficulty, he hadn't much time left. Farel should always remember their friendship; it had served God's church and they would both enjoy its fruits together in heaven.

Calvin held on another few weeks, dying finally on May 27, 1564. It was a good death by the standards of the day. He was in control of his faculties, and it was not violent or sudden but peaceful. According to his wishes, he was buried with no great pomp or ceremony and laid in an unmarked grave. Calvin worried about cults of remembrance.

Austere, in accordance with his reputation, even in death, Calvin left many accomplishments behind but little in the way of earthly goods. He distributed a small legacy among his nieces and nephews, the Academy, and the Genevan fund for refugees. His more enduring legacy would be apparent elsewhere, as he himself knew. In the final years, when an opponent wrote against him that the fact that he had been denied children was evidence of God's curse, Calvin recalled that little Jacques, the child Idelette had given birth to prematurely, had indeed died. Was this a sign of God's disfavor? No, replied Calvin, defiantly, "In Christendom I have ten thousand children."

The estimate may well have been too conservative.

Chapter Five

Calvin's Children

Claims for Calvin's influence in the modern world often sound like hyperbole. According to some versions, anyone who has been a participant in the modern Western experience is one of Calvin's children. You are, even if you think you're not! It is hard to sustain some of the more far-reaching accounts. (For instance, Calvin can hardly be held responsible for reality TV, Donald Trump, or the *Chicken Soup for the Soul* series.) But it is hard to deny that the impact both of the theology he formulated and of the movement he helped to found has been broad and deep, shaping many aspects of modern life and religion. Let us look first at some of the theories scholars have put forward about Calvin's influence on modern society before turning to his specifically theological and religious legacy.

Calvinism Distilled: The Spirit of Capitalism?

Perhaps the best-known theory about Calvin's influence on modernity is the so-called Weber thesis. Developed by the German sociologist Max Weber in 1905, it held that the Reformation—and Calvin and Calvinism in particular—contributed materially to the rise of modern capitalism. A number of Calvin's teachings—especially his (and Luther's) notion of a Christian, worldly calling and the idea of predestination—helped to create a sober, rational, and industrious breed of merchant capitalists that laid the foundation for modern, orderly forms of capitalism. Weber thought that Calvin's predestinarian doctrine was especially important in this. Calvinists who accepted this teaching and who were anxious about their eternal destiny looked for signs of their election and found them in their capacity to bring forth good fruit. An aspect of this fruitfulness was worldly success. And so, thought Weber, a good deal of "religious" energy, in the wake of Calvin, went into the formation of profitable enterprises and the investment (rather than consumption) of capital. This was in contrast to the strictures on wealth and the creation of profit characteristic of medieval Christianity. The successful medieval businessman always had a guilty conscience, but the early modern Calvinist businessman believed he was contributing to God's glory (and showing himself to be one of the saints) through his worldly success.

Was Weber right? Historians usually say no—or not exactly. Weber's evidence was thin and some of it was weak, and so he left himself open to all sorts of attacks on one detail or another. But what of Calvin's role in the development Weber lays out? Calvin never taught a simplistic scheme for the assurance of anxiety, and he did not say much that would have directly encouraged his followers to go out and generate wealth. In fact, Calvin was a regular and energetic critic of the businesspersons of Geneva, who, he felt, were interested only in their own gain. The impulse to generate profit could lead to social suicide, Calvin thought. And yet, on the other hand, he did provide a theological rationale for the loaning of money at interest, justifying current business practices and challenging the notion of medieval Christian ethics that these practices were "usurious" and therefore forbidden by the Bible and church law. Weber was right to note that Calvin had suggested that one's good works, while not at all the basis for salvation, could help to build a person's confidence that he was elect (although he emphasized more the solution of looking to Christ rather than oneself for such assurance). But there is not much evidence to suggest that Calvin could have counseled a parishioner to take comfort in the success of his business. Worldly goods were not necessarily an indication of God's favor. In fact, poverty, disease, and persecution were all cited by Calvin as trials visited on the saints by God who refines them in this earthly life for an eternal life of blessedness.

So, in a sense, the jury is still out on Weber. He is easy to contradict on the small stuff, but the larger thesis still seems to have some life to it, if only because it seems to fit with so many popular conceptions of Calvinist order, industry, and frugality. Calvin himself and his ideas did contribute toward the idea that work in the world was not only religiously valuable but was a religious imperative. Calvin feared idleness, and his followers were likewise energetic in their worldly activity. So there certainly seems to have been a work ethic encouraged by Calvinism, although it was by no means limited to this movement. (The Calvinist ethic, needless to say, is worlds away from the "greed is good" ethic of latter-day capitalism. So we should banish from our minds any sense that Calvin or an early Calvinist could have recognized the predatory practices of late modern financial wheeling and dealing as a reflection of a religious vocation.)

A most important contribution to economic and other aspects of modern life was Calvin's rejection of the idea, common in his time, that the world was just about at an end. Calvinists settled down in history. They felt we would be around for a while. And so, in contrast to groups who believed history was about finished and that there was little point in contributing to a decaying world, Calvin and Calvinists believed that God intended for Christians (and had chosen them!) to transform the world. This conviction, together with their work ethic, probably helped to unleash the dynamic involvement of Calvinists in economic, social, and political life; and it explains why Calvinists, even when in the minority, played a disproportionately large role in the formation of modern Western culture.

Calvinist Political Animals

Another one of those persistent ideas about Calvin's influence is the notion that somehow he profoundly affected modern politics. The number of potential sources in Calvin's thought and life to support the notion is seemingly endless, but we can point to just a few of the more significant ones.

First, it is noteworthy that Calvinists, after Calvin's death, were some of the more influential proponents of a right to resist (even violently) unjust rulers. Was Calvin in some sense an inspiration for sixteenth-century rebellions in Scotland, France, and the Netherlands? Might he be a source for the later American and French Revolutions? And if he was, how was he? Those who suggest that he might have been point to the way his thought encouraged Christians not to compromise with the governments they lived under when those governments required them to violate God's laws. There seems to be something in this. Calvin and a number of his contemporaries challenged the current idea that one could always (or usually) expect a perfect harmony between what God willed and what a ruler did or commanded. In fact, the experience of Calvinists living under repressive Catholic regimes convinced them that the opposite was more likely to be the case. But, unlike their contemporary Anabaptists, they would not take the option of saying, This government is bad because *all* governments are bad; we simply have to endure the suffering and separate ourselves, as best we can, from the surrounding non-Christian society. They believed government *shouldn't* be bad; it should reflect God's will, even if it doesn't right now. The crucial question that came next was, Can we do anything to change this government so that it *does* come closer to reflecting God's will? Here Calvinists were not of one mind. Calvin thought ordinary citizens couldn't do anything on their own, although they could participate in a movement of resistance under a leader whose constitutional role was to provide just this resistance. Other Calvinists interpreted in their own way Calvin's insistence against compromise, and they refused to obey—to the point of active and sometimes violent disobedience—rulers they viewed as ungodly. They probably also noticed that what he had said about signs and things in the sacraments (the sign—the bread of the Supper—is not to be confused with the thing it points to—Jesus Christ) could also apply to kings (their earthly authority is not to be confused with the transcendent power of God). And so Calvin's followers participated in a variety of revolutionary movements—late in his life, after his death, and on down into the period of the revolutions of the eighteenth and nineteenth centuries.

But Calvinism was not only implicated in revolution. It also played a role, or so some suggest, in the emergence of modern, Western political structures. For a long time, scholars have claimed that Calvin and his followers helped to introduce democracy to the modern world. The only problem with that contention is that in the sixteenth century, when Calvin lived, democracy was a frightening concept to many educated people of a certain social class. The fairly recent idea of "one person, one vote" would have seemed to Calvin hardly distinguishable from mob rule. On the other hand, when Calvin came to Geneva, he entered a republic that had a representative form of government. The vote was limited to certain persons, native-born male citizens and bourgeois (new arrivals in the city who generally paid for this status and the privilege of voting). Those who could vote elected leaders who served on the city's various deliberative bodies. The representative system and the limited franchise created what Calvin referred to as a mixture of aristocracy and democracy. This, to Calvin, was a sensible way of organizing government. The democratic element placed a brake on the overextension and the unjust use of power that is a common affliction of monarchy. And the aristocratic element would put qualified persons of good judgment into positions of authority, avoiding rule by the rabble. This aristocratic preference falls short of contemporary notions of democracy, but it is not very far removed from the vision of the majority of the American so-called founding fathers (who also feared radical forms of democracy).

Even more influential than Calvin's explicit reflection on civil government was the way he contributed to the organization of the Calvinist churches. In Geneva, the life of the church was overseen by deliberative bodies—the Company of Pastors and the (more-or-less representative) board of elders or consistory. We have seen that when Calvin's vision of the church was transplanted elsewhere, a more intricate model of a hierarchy of bodies—from local consistory (or session), to regional presbyteries (or classes), to a national synod (or general assembly)—was devised. Part of the rationale for this polity derived from Calvin's understanding of sin and its continuing effects. That is, we are all sinful, and we can be confident that individuals in the church—even those who make their way into the hierarchy—will continue to exhibit their sinful nature. So deliberative bodies served as a check upon the limited vision and the sinfulness of the individual. In Geneva and elsewhere, Calvin helped to introduce the practice of mutual correction. Members of pastoral bodies would sit around the table and point out each others' pertinent faults and failures. That may not sound like a fun evening, but it was intended to provide a way of seeing in oneself what others see and, in the process, to facilitate the amending of individual faults. It also illustrates the principle that we need each other—a variety of judgments and points of view—when we set about the process of decision making and governing. These principles were not that difficult to translate from church government to civil government. The systems of government adopted in the American colonies, and subsequently in the American republic, provide a vivid example of how this was done. The democratic element eventually became more pronounced, both in Calvinist churches and in the Calvinist-inspired systems of government, but the essential principles of representative government remain more or less as they were first envisioned in the sixteenth century.

These are just some of the areas that have been proposed as places where Calvin's influence has shaped modern life. There are, of course, other possible areas. For example, Calvin helped to transform the French language (and, through translation, other European languages), creating a simpler, clearer, and more direct way of communicating. This transformation might very well have paved the way, so some have argued, for the ways of thinking that made modern forms of philosophy possible, beginning in the century after Calvin. Also, Calvin's attack on the Catholic sacramental view of the world and nature (the idea that the world is suffused with the sacred) might have contributed to what Max Weber called "the disenchantment of the world"—the disappearance of magical beliefs and the advent of new, rationalistic interpretations of the world. This might also have contributed to the rise of modern science. And Calvin's view that biblical language was God's accommodated speech could also have helped to remove some of the potential obstacles in the Bible's narratives to free, scientific inquiry. (For example, the idea that the earth has to be the center of the universe because that is the ancient cosmology reflected in the Bible could be challenged, using Calvin's approach to interpretation, by saying that God's use of a cosmology in a biblical narrative is not the same as divine verification of that cosmology as scientifically true.)[13] All these are possible areas of influence. Let's turn now to Calvin's religious and theological heirs, where the influence is less ambiguous.

Orthodox Bulbs and a Tulip Harvest

Calvin's nearest immediate successors are sometimes not viewed as successors at all. That is, many have questioned whether they were really faithful interpreters of the theology he practiced. Theodore Beza, Calvin's first successor in Geneva, is one of these. He represents a broad group of Calvinists who, because they helped to found schools to perpetuate the Reformed theological legacy, are frequently called Reformed scholastics. Their approach is also sometimes labeled Reformed (or Calvinist) orthodoxy. They lived in a time when it had become increasingly important to defend one's theological insights by devising systems of theological thought that would be impervious to attack by Christians of another persuasion. As part of their defensive arsenal they used tools Calvin himself neglected. The philosophy of Aristotle was one such tool, a rigorously logical method of argument was another, and a deductive approach to theological reasoning was yet another. Whereas Calvin's method relied on rhetorical means of persuasion, his scholastic heirs tended to rely on logical proof.

This shift in method was reflected in a shift in the emphasis given to certain doctrines. Reformed scholastics tended to begin their presentations of Christian faith with a proof of the divine origin of Scripture. Once the divinity of the Bible had been established, it was thought, other elements of the theological system could be deduced from it. They also emphasized, more strongly than had Calvin, the doctrine of predestination. Since, as Calvin had seen, this was a doctrine that usefully underlined human reliance on God's grace and the sovereignty of God over all life, they tended to be impatient to get to the doctrine early on in their theological systems. While Calvin thought the doctrine needed to be set in the context of our reflection on how grace comes to us, many of his successors believed that predestination was so important that it should be a part of our first reflections on the being of God. The eternal decrees of God, after all, happened "before" creation, the fall of Adam and Eve, and the coming of Jesus Christ. Why not, then, start the whole story off with this doctrine?

The prominence given to predestination is apparent in the events that led to the first definition of a system of orthodox Calvinist doctrine at the Synod of Dordrecht in the Netherlands in 1618. It all started when a Dutch Calvinist pastor by the name of Jacobus Arminius (1560–1609) began to raise questions about this doctrine. He worried that a flat denial of the freedom of human beings to do anything for their salvation led people to be morally complacent. When he began to modify Calvinist doctrine by arguing that when God offered grace to persons they had the freedom to accept it or reject it and that God's eternal decree was a decision to save those who would believe, he gained a considerable following in the Netherlands. On the other hand, he provoked a heated response from the defenders of Calvinist orthodoxy, who felt that in this revision he had betrayed the entire tendency of Reformed Protestant thinking.

What did Arminius accomplish in this challenge to the late sixteenth-century views he had inherited? He had given more scope to human freedom and responsibility than Calvin had. He also had absolved God of the charge Bolsec said God was liable to if one adopted Calvin's scheme—namely, that God is the author of sin. (Humans bear responsibility for sin, since God's decree does not ordain sin but simply relates to what human beings do of their own accord.) The cost of these gains, however, was the loss of Calvin's notion that God's grace is always supreme in human affairs. Arminius believed that grace is an offer humans *can* refuse.

The Synod of Dordrecht's mostly Dutch delegates quickly condemned the teachings of Arminius and set about adopting the five classic tenets of orthodox Calvinism, easily remembered according to their first initials that spell out (in English) a flower that was all the rage in seventeenth-century Holland.[14]

    T = Total depravity
    U = Unconditional election
    L = Limited atonement
    I = Irresistible grace
    P = Perseverance of the saints

This was an affirmation of the Calvinism that had already become standard fare in the Reformed schools of the period. But it was a bit more than a simple reaffirmation of what Calvin had taught. For the first time, a Calvinist church body declared that Christ died only for the elect (limited atonement). Depending on how you interpret Calvin, he either did not teach this or he left the matter unclear (perhaps because the Bible doesn't state the matter clearly). The effect of Dordrecht's TULIP, however, was clear: Predestination was placed front and center in orthodox Calvinism, and the idea that human beings have the freedom to cooperate with God's grace was forever banished.

Scholars are divided on the question of whether the approaches of the Reformed scholastics and the definitions of orthodoxy are a departure from Calvin or a natural development of his thought. According to those who take the developmental view, Calvin's successors kept the content of Calvin's theology and simply modified some of his methods. For those who see a sharp departure, the change in method amounted to a change in content. Calvin resisted scholastic theological methods and the heavy use of philosophy because he wanted to draw his readers into the world of the Bible rather than into a rigid theological system designed to protect biblical truth.

Men (and Women) in Black

The most potent dose of Calvinism to find its way into the American bloodstream was administered by some of the first European immigrants to the New World—those who arrived on the shores of New England in the early seventeenth century. The Puritans were English Calvinists, but those who made their way across the Atlantic devised, over time, a definitively American (and, some say, paradigmatic) form of Calvinism.

Their religious inclinations mirrored Calvin's in several ways. First, like him, they were concerned to relate knowledge of God to knowledge of self, and so they paid close attention to inner religious experience. Puritan interest in matters of the heart, or the affections, intensified Calvin's own interest in how the Holy Spirit's work becomes manifest in an individual life. With Calvin also, this attention to the heart did not neglect the mind. Puritans believed in the value and necessity of education to refine the intellect so that persons could serve God as whole, complete individuals. Second, the Puritans adopted more than a little of Calvin's combative style. Reacting strongly against the conservative environment of the Church of England, they made the struggle against liturgical vestiges of Catholicism and the rule of bishops a centerpiece of their program for reform. In fact, Puritan militancy went a good deal further than Calvin was willing to go; he had no objection to England's episcopal system and was more accommodating of a variety of liturgical forms and worship practices than they were. Third, Puritan religion reflected Calvin's zeal for embodying faith in society and culture. The piety of the Puritans was not individualistic. Like Calvin, they believed that Christians were called upon to build a community of faith that would transform the world. The Puritan migration to New England was a piece of this world-transforming mission. Their enterprise was to build a New Jerusalem, which would be, in the words of one of their leaders, "as a City upon a Hill" (cf. Matt. 5:14). It was a new social project, this voyage to a new world, but it drew its inspiration from the old world experiment of Calvin's Geneva. It drew also from Calvinist understandings of a providential and predestining God, one who had chosen them and called them to be a special people, the instruments of God's mission to the broader world.

The Puritan sense of call and quest for social holiness is an important feature of Calvin's bequest to the modern world. Although in time the Puritans, in common with many other utopians before and since, failed to meet their own standards of success, their project did not end with their absorption into the bustling commercial culture of New England. It is more likely (as many have suggested) that their zeal for righteousness became sublimated in the American psyche and continues to manifest itself in a variety of ways, religious and secular. To this day, most Americans think of their nation as one that is distinct, one that ought to serve as a model for the world. One could argue that American politics (right and left certainly, but also elements of the center) are suffused with the influence of a Puritan Calvinist zeal for creating a new community of justice and righteousness (a New Deal? New Frontier? New Society?). Many of today's political actors, whether professional politicians or grassroots activists on the street with placards—be they Protestant, Catholic, Jewish, or agnostic—are likely true children of the Puritans and the Genevan reformer who inspired them.

The Critical Spirit in a Liberal Mode

Calvin lived before the dawn of the modern world, before the full flowering of a scientific and philosophical revolution that would revolutionize understandings of human being, nature, and history. Because his intellectual world was, as is sometimes said, "precritical" (meaning he lacked the advanced critical tools modern science, history, and the social sciences would provide), his intellectual accomplishments are frequently contrasted to those who lived in an age of criticism and who embraced critical tools. And so the theological movement that first accommodated modern science and philosophy—Protestant liberalism—might seem to be diametrically opposed to the spirit of Calvinism.

But is this fair? Those who think it isn't fair can point to the role played by the man often called "the father of modern theology"—the German preacher and theologian Friedrich Schleiermacher (1768–1834). Schleiermacher was a member of the Reformed Church, and he placed himself in the lineage of John Calvin. There are many elements of his theology that reflect Calvin's own outlook. Like Calvin (and the Puritans), he placed enormous stress on the religious affections; for him, they were the touchstone of all theological reflection. With Calvin, the doctrine of God's providence was highlighted, to the point where religion was defined as a feeling of "absolute dependence" upon God. But nowhere is the Calvinist and Reformation heritage more evident than in Schleiermacher's insistence that theological teachings inherited from earlier times are not immune from criticism. The critical spirit Calvin exemplified in his attacks on Catholic religious practices and scholastic theology was alive and well in the new theology Schleiermacher pioneered at the beginning of the nineteenth century.

Calvin's critical approach was well summarized in the Calvinist motto for the church adopted by a generation following his: *Ecclesia reformata, semper reformanda* ("The church reformed, always requiring reformation"). The idea was that the church could never be content with itself and its own present understandings. The church's doctrine and life should be subjected to continual criticism supplied by the careful reading of Scripture, interpreted with the aid of the Holy Spirit. Because this practice of criticism was always carried out with a deep sense of reverence for the Bible, the critical approach of Schleiermacher and his liberal successors, who turned their critical tools on that very biblical text, has sometimes seemed out of step with Calvinist inclinations. Liberals used historical criticism to demonstrate, among other things, that Moses could not have written the first five books of the Bible (as tradition held and as Calvin assumed), that Paul did not write every letter that bears his name, and that much of what is included in the Gospel accounts of Jesus' life is not reliable as history.

Can one really view a movement that seems to have launched a frontal assault on the Bible as a reflection of Calvin's legacy? If one views liberalism as an attack on the Bible, probably not. Most liberals, however (Schleiermacher included), did not think that critical interpretation of Scripture was an attack on the Bible. Instead, for them, to read the Bible critically was a measure of one's serious interest in the text itself. Critical methods were not used to demolish a sense of biblical authority but to understand the text better in all its meanings. Looked at from this point of view, the critical approach of liberal biblical scholars was not terribly different from the humanist-inspired approach Calvin himself used. He employed the best critical methods available in his time, just as Schleiermacher and his successors used the methods they had at hand.

Marking the Fundamentals: Calvinist Conservation

Not everyone is so easily convinced that the liberal approach is consistent with the historic affirmations of Christianity or consonant with Calvin's contribution to theology. Among the most skeptical were a group of nineteenth and early twentieth-century American theologians, Charles Hodge (1797–1878), Benjamin Warfield (1851–1921), and A. A. Hodge (1823–1886), who taught at Princeton Seminary and were known as the founders of the "Princeton theology." The Princetonians were, as they understood it, orthodox Calvinists, and they were vociferous critics of both the liberal treatment of Scripture and liberalism's sacrificing of certain historical doctrines they believed were essential to the Christian faith. For many years, they fostered among American Calvinist evangelicals a systematic version of Reformed orthodoxy while they fought a rearguard action against the supposedly dangerous innovations of the liberals. The idea that Scripture is without error of any kind became the centerpiece of their program. Although Hodge and his students believed that this understanding of Scripture went back to Calvin, in fact the chief source for their view was the seventeenth-century Genevan theologian François Turretin (1623–1687) and his account of the verbal inspiration of the Bible.

The Princeton theology was one of the chief engines behind the formation of an antiliberal movement that in the early twentieth century came to be called fundamentalism (because of its proponents' arguments for defining and preserving certain doctrinal "fundamentals," which, if sacrificed, would subvert Christian faith). Fundamentalism was marked by attacks on persons thought to be guilty of evangelical "heresy" (because of their views of biblical authority), on scientific theories believed to be in conflict with biblical teaching (notably evolution), and on social and political programs thought to contradict Christian values (socialism and communism).

Was Calvin, then, a source for modern fundamentalism? It would seem so. Calvinists, at any rate, counted themselves among the defenders of Christian fundamentals such as biblical inerrancy. However, Calvinists of quite another sort found themselves on the other side in the great "civil war" that afflicted (and continues to afflict) modern Protestantism. Did one side have a stronger claim to stand in the tradition of Calvin? An answer to that question almost inevitably betrays one's party affiliation. To take a middle path, one might say that aspects of Calvin were reflected in both movements. Protestant liberalism mirrored the critical and revolutionary aspect, while the Princeton theology and fundamentalism reflected a conservative version—the zealous and able defender of the faith against its detractors. Neither were simple replications of Calvin, since the insights of Calvin's theology of the sixteenth century inevitably required translation and adjustment when applied to new and different circumstances.

A New Orthodoxy

In the early and middle part of the twentieth century, a new theological movement that drew inspiration from Calvin and other sixteenth-century reformers helped to overcome the impasse of the liberal-fundamentalist controversy and provided, for a time, a powerful theological consensus. At the center of this movement was the Swiss (and Reformed) theologian Karl Barth (1886–1968). Barth began his theological career rejecting decisively what he saw as the "wrong turn" of theological liberalism. In his view, liberalism had accommodated theology to culture and confused God's word with human words. He found fault, particularly, in the tendency of Schleiermacher and others to base theology on human experience. Liberals, he thought, had neglected the biblical doctrine of revelation that Luther and Calvin had so zealously defended. His task, as he saw it, was to restore revelation to its proper role. In this task, Barth and his followers differed from the fundamentalists. For the former, the Bible was not God's word because it is free from all error. (Barth thought there was plenty of error in the Bible.) It was God's word because it points to Jesus Christ, the one Word of God. Although Barth's early theology of God's "wholly otherness" owed more to the Danish existentialist philosopher Søren Kierkegaard than to any of the sixteenth-century reformers, as he moved increasingly toward emphasizing the centrality of Jesus Christ in all theological reflection, he drew inspiration from Calvin. But the Calvin

Barth drew upon was a Barthian Calvin, one who supplied him with ammunition to be used against the liberal tendency to build theology on the foundation of human experience. Where Calvin's theology was less than explicit in its support of his position (such as in his reflection on the natural knowledge of God), Barth argued that Calvin could do with some minor correction. At other points, such as predestination, Barth felt free to say that Calvin had plainly got it wrong. God is an electing God, according to Barth. But in his view, Calvin had misconstrued predestination because he had failed to see clearly the implications of a Christ-centered view of God. The predestining God we see in Jesus Christ is Christ himself—one who, instead of rejecting humanity (or some portion of humanity), bears the pain of rejection and shows the face of the gracious God in whom all humanity is elect. Barth's theology, taking seriously the concentration on grace inherited from Augustine and reflected in Calvin, was a theology in which grace was the first and last word.

Barth's theology helped to stimulate an enormous amount of interest in Calvin's thought in the middle of the twentieth century. Those who found themselves in Barth's circle, or in closely allied theological movements, believed he had rescued the thought of Calvin and other classical theologians from the oblivion to which the liberal tradition (as they thought) had consigned them. Among Barth's allies in a movement that came to be known as neo-orthodoxy were the American theologians Reinhold Niebuhr (1892–1971) and H. Richard Niebuhr (1894–1963). The Niebuhrs, who also belonged to the Reformed tradition, shared Barth's concern about the cul-de-sac into which liberalism had led theology. But, partly because the American reception of Calvinism had included a more positive assessment of human experience as a theological source, their opposition to strands in the liberal tradition was not nearly as vociferous or unequivocal as Barth's. H. Richard Niebuhr in particular, strongly influenced by American theologian Jonathan Edwards's (1703–1758) interpretations of divine holiness and the human affections and by the historical theology of the liberal Ernst Troeltsch (1865–1923), managed a unique synthesis of liberal and Barthian themes. In the emphasis the Niebuhrs placed on the doctrines of God's sovereignty and human sin, in their accounts of revelation and faith, in contributions to Christian ethical reflection, and in their active engagement with issues of current concern (socialism, pacifism, and the civil rights movement), they reflected important elements of Calvin's theological and religious legacy.[15]

Liberating Theology

In the late twentieth century, the neo-orthodox consensus began to break down, giving way to a number of theological movements, none of which achieved a position of dominance. However, one tendency was especially noteworthy, and that was the appearance of theologies that focused, from one or another angle, on the theme of the liberation of human beings from conditions of oppression. Liberation theologies from Latin American, Africa, and Asia; feminist theology; African American theology—although they differed in particulars—shared many common features. Is Calvin's theology implicated in some way in the approaches taken by those who interpreted Christian faith within these new theological frameworks?

Perhaps. At least there are certain Calvinist predilections that emerge when one examines features of the liberation-oriented approaches. First, with Calvin, these approaches do not overlook sin. They define sin in ways that Calvin perhaps would not recognize, but they share with him the insight that sin (whether defined in Calvin's traditional terms or viewed as structural facts, such as racism or sexism) is a stubborn and enduring feature of human experience. Second, the critical spirit Calvin reflected is a feature of liberation theology. In all forms, theologies of this sort attempt to name the sin that stands as a barrier to authentic expressions of human wholeness. The naming of sin in almost every case involves a criticism of culture, of church structures, and of inherited ways of doing theology. Calvin's sense of his freedom and responsibility to engage in prophetic critique of religion, theology, and culture, then, is echoed in liberation theologies. Third, just as Calvin was not content to let the Christian message apply only to the salvation of individual souls but believed that the Bible's vision of a community of justice and righteousness was a call to Christian action, liberation theologians also seek to give an account of Christian faith that is socially embodied, that challenges violent and dehumanizing practices, and that lives out patterns of justice. Finally, liberation approaches reflect something of the passion common to the theological and religious heirs of Calvin. Calvin's children never shrank from the task of changing their world for the better. Liberationists, if not in every case direct descendants of Calvin, have in common with him and his heirs the prophetic edge and hopeful confidence of Christians throughout the ages who have believed that the founding of a visible city of God is a task to which each one is called.[16]

Lines of Descent

We have looked at a wide array of cultural developments and a curious assortment of religious heirs. Can these all together be thought of as Calvin's offspring? If so, Calvin's claim to have fathered ten thousand children was a serious miscalculation. But perhaps some in the crowd are illegitimate children? In cases such as these, legitimacy and illegitimacy, like beauty, are in the eye of the beholder. I have tried to point to some of the more important genetic traits that have been passed down to a now very diverse, and certainly dysfunctional, Calvinist family. But, sorry to say, the evidence we have doesn't approach the accuracy of a theological DNA sample from the man himself. Given this level of uncertainty, and the incredibly diverse collection of heirs, one might wonder whether we have the genealogy right. Is it possible that a Christian feminist and a Christian fundamentalist can share a family tree? And, if it is possible, what in the world does this tell us about their common ancestor?

It might be the case, as some have suggested, that Calvin's legacy is so complex, even confused, because of the complexity of Calvin himself. On the one hand, he was the humanist who criticized the rigid and lifeless dogma of his time, who counseled flexibility and tolerance, and who argued for an openness to mystery. On the other hand, he was a man fearful of a chaotic age that lacked an organizing structure, a conservative who struggled vigorously to impose order on a disordered world. Calvin was, in a certain sense, a man at odds with himself. Perhaps it is this internal tension that we have to thank for the unruly brood who are Calvin's surviving heirs.[17]

Whatever our judgment on Calvin's psyche, it is clear that his legacy is a rich one. Calvin's beneficiaries are certainly not through with him. As the modern West gives way to a postmodern and pluralistic successor and as Calvin's Reformed tradition finds fertile soil outside the West, particularly in Asia, the legacy will take on new forms. And so, as Calvinism marches on in many permutations and into new worlds Calvin can hardly have imagined, one may hope his heirs use his legacy for constructive ends. Or at least, given the history of Calvinist contentiousness, we may wish with Calvin that they "not discourage one another, or be an obstacle to one another, or make [themselves] hateful to one another."[18]

Notes

1. *Sermons on Micah by John Calvin*, trans. Blair Reynolds (Lewiston, NY: Mellen, 1990), 280, 285.
2. See the account in Richard Stauffer, *The Humanness of John Calvin* (Nashville: Abingdon, 1971), 43–46.
3. John Calvin, *Treatise on Relics*, in *Three French Treatises*, ed. Francis Higman (London: Athlone Press, 1970), 86.
4. Johann Eck, *Enchiridion of Commonplaces against Luther and Other Enemies of the Church* (1525), trans. Ford Lewis Battles (Grand Rapids: Baker, 1979), 12–13.
5. *Letters of John Calvin*, vol. 3, ed. Jules Bonnet (New York: Franklin, 1972), 359ff.
6. Dr. Seuss, *The Cat in the Hat* (Boston: Houghton Mifflin, 1957), 55.
7. See the hymn attributed to Calvin, "I Greet Thee Who My Sure Redeemer Art," *The Presbyterian Hymnal* (Louisville, KY: Westminster/John Knox, 1990), number 457.
8. John Newton wrote the hymn "Amazing Grace" around the year 1770.
9. John Calvin, commentary on Daniel 6:22, in *Daniel I*, trans. T. H. L. Parker (Grand Rapids: Eerdmans, 1993), 266. Calvin cites Acts 5:29 in his own translation in the final lines of his *Institutes of the Christian Religion*, ed. John T. McNeill, trans. Ford Lewis Battles (Philadelphia: Westminster Press, 1960), 1521.
10. The quotations are taken from John Fiske, *The Beginnings of New England or the Puritan Theocracy in Its Relations to Civil and Religious Liberty* (Boston and New York: Houghton Mifflin, 1894), 57–58f. Helpful discussions of the history of negative depictions of Calvin are found in Stauffer, *Humanness of John Calvin*, 19–31, and Thomas J. Davis, "Images of Intolerance: John Calvin in Nineteenth-Century History Textbooks," *Church History* 65, no. 2 (1996): 234–48.
11. Theodore Beza, *L'histoire de la vie et mort de Calvin*, in *Ioannis Calvini Opera quae supersunt omnia*, ed. Wilhelm Baum, Edward Cunitz, and Edward Reuss (Brunswick: C. A. Schwetschker, 1863–1900), vol. 21, col. 39–40.
12. Those Calvin called Spiritual Libertines were a group associated with Quintin of Hainaut (and sometimes called Quintinists). Their views were mystical and tinged with pantheism. They should not be confused with the Genevan political faction (the Perrinists) whom Calvin also called Libertines. "Nicodemite" was the term Calvin used

to describe persons who practiced religious dissimulation, believing that, when living under threat of persecution, one could, appropriately, hold evangelical views while appearing to be a conforming Catholic.
13. A version of this argument is made by B. A. Gerrish in his "The Reformation and the Rise of Modern Science: Luther, Calvin, and Copernicus," in *The Old Protestantism and the New: Essays on the Reformation Heritage* (Edinburgh: T. & T. Clark, 1982).
14. The mnemonic device TULIP was an English invention of a later age. While it conveniently calls to mind a flower associated with Holland, the seventeenth-century Dutch knew nothing of this particular way of summarizing the doctrine adopted at Dordrecht.
15. For an expanded account of both H. R. Niebuhr's and Barth's assessment of Calvin, as well as the controversy over whether Schleiermacher is a legitimate heir of the Genevan reformer, see my "Getting Calvin Right: How Karl Barth Changed Our Reading of the Reformer," *Princeton Seminary Bulletin* 30 (2009): 63–80.
16. Skeptics sometimes dismiss the claim that Latin American liberation theologians can be regarded as heirs of Calvin because the best-known figures in the movement were Catholic priests, seemingly indebted to other streams of religious and social thought. However, the first of the Latin Americans to employ the term "theology of liberation" was something of a direct descendant: the Brazilian Presbyterian Rubem Alves, whose 1968 Princeton Theological Seminary dissertation, "Toward a Theology of Liberation," was published with the title *A Theology of Human Hope* (Washington: Corpus, 1969). Alves was an important voice, and his insights were reflected in both Protestant and Catholic streams of liberation theology.
17. This is the argument of William J. Bouwsma, *John Calvin: A Sixteenth-Century Portrait* (New York: Oxford University Press, 1988). See also Suzanne Selinger, *Calvin against Himself: An Inquiry in Intellectual History* (Hamden, CT: Archon Books, 1984).
18. "Discours d'adieu aux mambres du Petit Conseil," *Ioannis Calvini Opera quae supersunt omnia*, vol. 9, col. 890.

Further Reading

The best introduction to Calvin's thought as he himself expressed it is his *Institutes of the Christian Religion*, which is available in a good English translation by Ford Lewis Battles, edited by John T. McNeill (Philadelphia: Westminster, 1960). An equally good way to see Calvin's thinking "in movement" is to look at his biblical commentaries. An outdated translation is available in a complete set: *Calvin's Commentaries*, 22 vols. (Grand Rapids: Baker, 1984). Also available are select titles in newer series with more up-to-date translations: *Calvin's Old Testament Commentaries*, ed. David Wright (Grand Rapids: Eerdmans, 1993–); *Calvin's New Testament Commentaries*, ed. David W. Torrance and Thomas F. Torrance (Grand Rapids: Eerdmans, 1994). For a useful introduction to Calvin as a biblical expositor, see T. H. L. Parker's *Calvin's Old Testament Commentaries* (Louisville, KY: Westminster/John Knox, 1993) and *Calvin's New Testament Commentaries* (Louisville, KY: Westminster/John Knox, 1993). Sadly, few useful English translations of Calvin's sermons are currently available, but T. H. L. Parker's *Calvin's Preaching* (Louisville, KY: Westminster/John Knox, 1992) is a helpful introduction to his homiletic practice.

Several fine biographies of Calvin are readily available. See especially T. H. L. Parker, *John Calvin: A Biography* (Philadelphia: Westminster, 1975); Alister E. McGrath, *A Life of John Calvin: A Study in the Shaping of Western Culture* (Oxford: Basil Blackwell, 1990); and Bruce Gordon, *Calvin* (New Haven: Yale University Press, 2009). In addition, some general studies of Calvin's thought may serve as a useful introduction. See especially William J. Bouwsma,

John Calvin: A Sixteenth-Century Portrait (New York: Oxford University Press, 1988) and François Wendel, *Calvin: Origins and Development of His Religious Thought* (Grand Rapids: Baker, 1996).

For specialized studies in Calvin's theology, the reader might begin with a sampling of the following: Ford Lewis Battles, *Interpreting John Calvin* (Grand Rapids: Baker, 1996); Edward A. Dowey Jr., *The Knowledge of God in Calvin's Theology* (Grand Rapids: Eerdmans, 1994); B. A. Gerrish, *Grace and Gratitude: The Eucharistic Theology of John Calvin* (Minneapolis: Augsburg Fortress, 1993); Susan E. Schreiner, *The Theater of His Glory: Nature and the Thought of John Calvin* (Grand Rapids: Baker, 1989); and David Steinmetz, *Calvin in Context* (New York: Oxford University Press, 1995).

Calvin's relation to the intellectual ferment and political developments of his time is examined in a number of helpful studies. See Carlos M. N. Eire, *War against the Idols* (Cambridge: Cambridge University Press, 1986); Christopher Elwood, *The Body Broken: The Calvinist Doctrine of the Eucharist and the Symbolization of Power in Sixteenth-Century France* (New York: Oxford University Press, 1999); Mark Greengrass, *The Reformation in France* (Oxford: Basil Blackwell, 1987); Robert M. Kingdon, *Adultery and Divorce in Calvin's Geneva* (Cambridge, MA: Harvard University Press, 1995) and *Geneva and the Coming of the Wars of Religion in France, 1555–1563* (Geneva: Librairie Droz, 1956); Raymond A. Mentzer, *Sin and the Calvinists: Morals Control and the Consistory in the Reformed Tradition*, Sixteenth Century Essays and Studies 32 (Kirksville, MO: Sixteenth Century Journal Publishing, 1994); E. William Monter, *Calvin's Geneva* (New York: John Wiley & Sons, 1967); and William Naphy, *Calvin and the Consolidation of the Genevan Reformation* (Manchester: Manchester University Press, 1994).

For works that deal with subjects related to Calvin's impact on subsequent historical developments, see W. Fred Graham, ed., *Later Calvinism: International Perspectives* (Kirksville, MO: Truman State University Press, 1993); Francis Higman, *The Style of John Calvin in His French Polemical Treatises* (Oxford: Oxford University Press, 1957); John T. McNeill, *The History and Character of Calvinism* (New York: Oxford University Press, 1954); Richard A. Muller, *Christ and the Decree: Christology and Predestination in Reformed Theology from Calvin to Perkins* (Grand Rapids: Baker, 1986); Menna Prestwich, ed., *International Calvinism, 1541–1715* (Oxford: Clarendon, 1985); Robert V. Schnucker, ed., *Calviniana: Ideas and Influence of John Calvin* (Kirksville, MO: Sixteenth Century Journal Publishers, 1988); Keith

Thomas, *Religion and the Decline of Magic* (New York: Scribner, 1971); and Michael Walzer, *The Revolution of the Saints: A Study in the Origins of Radical Politics* (Cambridge, MA: Harvard University Press, 1965).

Index

accommodation. *See* revelation
affair of the placards, 7
Alciati, Andrea, 2, 3
Alves, Rubem, 88n16
Anabaptists, 52–53, 56, 58, 63, 73
Anselm of Canterbury, 21, 37–38
Aristotle, 76
Arminius, Jacobus, 77
Augustine, 4, 33, 43, 45, 50, 52, 55, 64, 83

baptism, 54, 56
Barth, Karl, 82–83
Bern, 10, 59, 64
Bernard of Clairvaux, 41
Beza, Theodore, 62–63, 68, 76
Bolsec, Jerome, 63–65, 67, 68, 77
Bucer, Martin, 12
Budé, Guillaume, 2
Bure, Idelette de, 12, 13, 70
Bush, George W., 30

Calvin, Gérard, 1–2
Calvin, John
  biblical commentaries of, 17
  Catechism of the Church of Geneva, 16, 49
  conversion, 5–6
  critics of, 62–63, 64, 70
  Ecclesiastical Ordinances, 12–13
  on economic life, 71–73
  education, 1–2, 3
  and France, xii, 14, 69
  and Geneva, 10–18, 68–69, 74–75
  iconoclasm of, 22–24, 54, 80, 84
  illness and death, 70
  influence of, xi–xii, 68–69, 70, 71–85
  on reformation, 15–18
  teaching of, 17, 69
  temperament, xii, 14, 62–63, 70
  and theological controversy, 62–68
Calvinism, xi–xii, 71–85
  and capitalism, 71–73
  and liberal democracy, 73–75
  and science, 75–76
  See also Reformed scholasticism
Capito, Wolfgang, 12
Carnegie, Dale, 11, 13
Carter, Jimmy, 30
Christian life, 43–45
church, 50–54
  government and discipline of, 11–13, 15–16, 52–54, 74–75
  marks of, 51–52
  offices of, 12–13, 16–17, 54
  and state, 58–61
  as visible and invisible, 50–51
civil government, 57–61, 73–75
  and rebellion, 60–61, 73–74
Clinton, Bill, 30
Consistory. *See* Church: government and discipline
Cop, Nicholas, 6
creation, 29. *See also* human being
Cyprian of Carthage, 51

determinism, 30–31
Donatists, 50–51, 52, 53
Dordrecht, Synod of, 77–78

Eck, Johann, 25
Edwards, Jonathan, 83
election. *See* predestination
Erasmus, Desiderius, 2, 6, 7, 34
eucharist, 54, 55, 57–58, 63, 74

evil, 29, 31–32. *See also* providence of God and evil

faith, 41–43, 49
Farel, Guillaume, 10–12, 66, 70
feminism, 84, 85
Fisher, Roger, 11
Francis I, 2, 6–7, 8, 60
fundamentalism, 81–82, 85

Geisel, Theodor (Dr. Seuss), 37
Geneva, 10–18, 68–69, 74–75, 79
   Academy of, 16–17, 68–69, 70
   magistrates of, 11–12, 12–14, 59, 61, 64–68, 70
   and religious refugees, 14
God
   knowledge of, 19–22, 25, 27–28, 32, 35
   revelation of (*see* revelation)
   as Trinity, 28–29, 65–66
   worship of, 21–24, 34
   wrath and love of, 39–40
   See also idolatry
grace, 4–5, 6, 40–41, 43–44, 46, 48–49, 50, 77–78, 83. *See also* justification, predestination

Hodge, A. A., 81
Hodge, Charles, 81–82
Holy Spirit, 26–27, 40–41, 42, 43–45, 78
human being
   as created, 21–22, 29
   as fallen, 32–35
   and freedom, 30–31, 34
   and God's image, 29, 33, 44
humanism, 2–3, 5, 6, 7–8, 17, 18, 27, 34, 68, 81, 85

idolatry, 21–24, 34, 54, 58
Institutes of the Christian Religion, 7–8, 9, 17–18, 19–61, 62

Jefferson, Thomas, 59
Jesus Christ
   as human and divine, 37–38
   as mediator, 34–35, 37–40
   as mirror of election, 49
   mystical union of believers with, 40–41
   offices of, 38–39
   and the work of redemption, 39–40
justification, 4, 41, 43–44

Kierkegaard, Søren, 82

law, 35–37
   uses of the, 35–36
Lefèvre d'Etaples, Jacques, 2, 6, 10
Le Franc, Jeanne, 1
l'Estoile, Pierre de, 2
liberation theology, 84
Libertines, 13–14, 63, 87n12
Lord's Supper. *See* Eucharist
Luther, Martin, x, 1–2, 3, 4–5, 6, 15, 19, 23, 25, 34, 41, 43, 55–56,. 57, 71, 82

Marcion, 36
Marguerite of Navarre, 2, 6
Medici, Catherine de, 69
Melanchthon, Philip, 35, 43
Michelangelo, 23–24
Mystical union. *See* Jesus Christ

neo-orthodoxy, 83, 84
Newton, John, 49
Nicodemites, 63, 87n12
Niebuhr, H. Richard, 83
Niebuhr, Reinhold, 83

Paine, Thomas, 58
Parlement of Paris, 18
Pelagius, 4, 33, 43, 64
Perrin, Ami, 14, 87n12
Pighius, Albertus, 34
politics. *See* civil government
predestination, 45–49, 63–65, 76–78, 83
Princeton theology, 81–82
Protestant liberalism, 79–81, 82, 83
providence of God, 30–32, 57–58, 61, 80
   and evil, 31–32
   and thankfulness, 58, 61
Puritans, 78–79

Reformation, 4–5, 15–18
Reformed scholasticism, 76–78

regeneration. *See* sanctification
Renée de France, Duchess of Ferrara, 9
repentance, 44. *See also* sanctification
revelation
    and authority, 25–27
    and rhetoric, 27–28
    rhetoric, 2–3, 21, 27–28, 76

sacraments, 43, 51–52, 54–57, 74
sanctification, 43–45
Savoy, Duchy of, 10–11
Schleiermacher, Friedrich, 80–81, 82, 88n15
scholasticism, 2, 3, 4, 8, 20, 64, 76–78, 80
Scripture
    authority of, 25–27, 81–82, 82–83
    interpretation of, 17, 36–37, 80
    as theological source, 25, 46–48, 53, 57–58, 65
    See also revelation
Seneca, 6
Servetus, Michael, 28–29, 63, 65–68
sin, 34–35, 37, 39–40, 43, 44

Sorbonne, 1–2, 3, 18
Springsteen, Bruce, 33
Stoicism, 30
Strasbourg, 9, 12
Sturm, Jean, 12

theology, 20–21
Thomas Aquinas, 45–46
Trinity. *See* God
Troeltsch, Ernst, 83
Trump, Donald, 71
Turretin, François, 81

Ury, William, 11

Warfield, Benjamin, 81
Wars of Religion, 9, 69
Weber, Max, 71–73, 75
Wolmar, Melchior, 3

Zwingli, Huldrych, x, 5, 55–56, 57, 59, 64–65

CPSIA information can be obtained
at www.ICGtesting.com
Printed in the USA
FFOW04n0003050317
33001FF

9 780664 262242